Weathering the
STORM

Christian Pacifist Responses to War

A collection of essays by various authors

Faith and Life Press, Newton, Kansas

Weathering the Storm: Christian Pacifist Responses to War offers guidance and encouragement, in the wake of the Persian Gulf War, for people who choose nonviolent means of solving conflict. In this collection of essays, various authors reflect on ways to make peace in the home, in school, in the workplace, in churches, in the community, and in the world.

Printed in the United States of America
94   93   92   91   4   3   2   1

Library of Congress Number 91-072445
International Standard Book Number 0-87303-149-0

Editorial direction for Faith and Life Press by Susan E. Janzen, general editor; copyediting by Edna Dyck; design by John Hiebert; printing by Mennonite Press.

Contents

How does the community of believers respond to war? What
factors determine the actions of a congregation? Here are the
stories of several Mennonite congregations.

Any war is fought on many fronts. Alongside the military battle
is a political battle. People also fight a battle of conscience and of
the soul to maintain faith. And it isn't easy, especially if they
stand alone.

Introduction
A People of God in Time of War

Duane K. Friesen

The community of believers, tested in the present time but living with the memory of a heritage and the hope of renewal and transformation yet to come, nurture and sustain each other.

Many Gifts, One Spirit

Now there are varieties of gifts, but the same Spirit; and there are varieties of service, but the same Lord; and there are varieties of working, but it is the same God who inspires them all in every one. To each is given the manifestation of the Spirit for the common good. (1 Cor. 12: 4-7)

War is like a refiner's fire. It tests our loyalties and commitments in the face of patriotic and nationalistic fervor. It tests our patience and hope, as we feel powerless before the engines of war. It tests our strength and endurance as we sorrow and grieve at the destruction of life, property, and the environment. It tests our love as we are accused by fellow citizens of disloyalty and cowardice.

In such times, one is grateful for the fellowship of believers: people who have experienced the powerful gift of God's love in Jesus Christ. This community of people, tested in the present time but living with the memory of a heritage, and the hope of renewal and transformation yet to come, nurture and sustain each other. As I read these essays, I was reminded of 1 Corinthians 12, which tells of the many gifts in the church. In these essays we receive the gifts of writers, teachers, professors, psychiatrists, pastors, church administrators, counselors, youth workers, peace activists—each enriching us and contributing to an awareness of our responsibilities as Christians. To be faithful, we depend upon each other, as each individual is moved by the Spirit of Christ for the sake of our common good.

Anguish as Resident Aliens

And when he drew near and saw the city he wept over it, saying, "Would that even today you knew the things that make for peace! But now they are hid from your eyes." (Luke 21:41-42)

Anguish and hope are the words that perhaps best characterize the essays in this volume. These are not essays which reflect the euphoria of military victory. A number of the writers speak of sorrow, grief, pain, even anger and frustration. Alan Moore-Beitler, pastor of the Hyattsville, Maryland, Mennonite congregation sums up the feelings of many: "Anger, sadness, frustration, feelings of despair and powerlessness, serious questions about the real nature and depth of our own commitment to peace and pacifism all came rushing to the surface from the days of December preceding the war through January and February."

But the authors of these essays are not cynical or bitter. Rather, they reflect a sorrow born out of compassion, out of a vision for another way to peace, out of the deep yearning and hope expressed in the words of Jesus: "Would that even today you knew the things that make for peace! But now they are hid from your eyes."

Katie Funk Wiebe and Doug Penner recall Psalm 137: "By the rivers of Babylon, there we sat down and we wept, when we remembered Zion. How can we sing the songs of Zion in a foreign land?"

The psalm has multilayered meanings. As we remember the exiles, at the time of Jeremiah, who were carried off to Babylon, our hearts weep for the orphans and thousands of refugees created by war. Babylon, the modern-day land of Iraq, is weeping. Iraq is a land devastated by war, a land, at this writing, in the midst of civil war. Kuwait is weeping—it is a country destroyed by war in order to save it. The earth is weeping as black smoke and oil pollute the air and water. Palestinians weep, as their freedom still remains only a dim hope.

And we weep as North American Christians, as the language of violence rather than words and actions of peace and reconciliation have overtaken our lands. As pacifist Christians, we feel like resident aliens in our own lands. We experience the alienation and separation from those around us. James Longacre identifies our internal struggle to balance our loyalty to Jesus Christ and citizenship in the context of the powerful symbols and rituals of patriotism. Norma Peters Duerksen describes how teachers in the public school struggle with what it means to be a witness in settings of overcharged patriotism, where the children they teach experience fear, confusion, and pain. Doug Penner gives us guidance on how to function as peacemakers in the workplace when we feel the emotional tension of wanting to maintain personal relationships with our co-workers, at the same time that we feel strongly about maintaining the integrity of our own pacifist beliefs. Dorothy Friesen reflects on how we befriend the enemy in times of war, when even our own fellow Arab citizens are harassed and dehumanized. Robert Hull describes Martin Buber's philosophy of "I-Thou" dialogue as a way to relate to neighbors with whom we disagree.

Jesus Christ, Our Lord

Let each of you look not only to your own interests, but to the interests of others. Let the same mind be in you that was in Christ Jesus, who, though he was in the form of God, did not regard equality with God as something to be exploited, but emptied himself, taking the form of a slave, being born in human likeness. And being found in human form, he humbled himself and became obedient to the point of death—even death on a cross. (Philippians 2:4-8)

The foundation of a Mennonite pacifist ethic is Jesus Christ. Mennonites confess the two central affirmations of the Nicene Creed: that in Jesus Christ, God's nature has been most supremely revealed, and the nature of our humanity has been most vividly modeled.

Paul's appeal to Christians to look not only after their own interests, but also the interests of others, is grounded in an understanding of the God revealed in Jesus Christ. Prayer to the God we know in Christ, is not just a prayer to protect "our own," but a prayer to sustain and nourish the lives of all human beings, including the Iraqi people and soldiers, even Saddam Hussein. Hubert Brown writes that in Christ he has discovered "the everlasting, merciful God who is reconciling the world into one." Roelf Kuitse applies this universal love to our relationship with Muslims. The Spirit of Christ overcomes our arrogance and empowers us to work at reconciliation—even in situations that appear hopeless.

But Katie Funk Wiebe also reminds us that times of war are no occasion for a kind of pacifist triumphalism. "Nonviolence has no glory either unless it reflects the Spirit of Christ." The spirit of humility is reflected in the congregation in Montreal which reports the linkage of prayer to reaching out their hands in friendship to their Arab and Jewish brothers and sisters in their own city who are experiencing the pain of the war. They quote Henri Nouwen: "Prayer—living in the presence of God—is the most radical peace action we can imagine" (Henri Nouwen, *Seeds of Hope*, Bantam, 1989).

Helmut Harder reminds us again of the heritage of the Anabaptist-Mennonite tradition, which has consistently based peacemaking in the example of Jesus Christ. The theme of the centrality of Christ runs through the Schleitheim Confession, the life and teachings of Menno Simons, the Dordrecht Confession of 1632, and the Ris Confession of 1766. A 1975 Mennonite Brethren Confession sums up the tradition well: "The Christian seeks to practice Christ's law of love in all situations, including those involving personal injustice, social upheaval, and international tensions."

Unmasking the Powers

He disarmed the principalities and powers and made a public example of them, triumphing over them in him. (Colossians 2:15)

Why do we grieve rather than rejoice? Why cannot we simply sit back and enjoy the fruits of a military victory like so many of our fellow citizens? Roelf Kuitse reminds us of the history of bitter enmity between the "Christian" West and our Muslim neighbors. How do we as Christians build a new relationship? George Dyck points out how as descendants of Cain we deceive ourselves with our own self-righteousness, ignore our own selfishness and greed, and project total evil upon our enemy. Can we find an alternative before we destroy ourselves?

James Harder calls our attention to the negative economic consequences of a permanent war economy. He points out that the high technology Persian Gulf War was made possible by the huge military expenditures during the Reagan presidency. Hubert Brown urges us to reflect upon the impact of our choices as each dollar for military hardware and war robs the poor of basic necessities. What are our responsibilities as citizens to speak and act on behalf of the poor and dispossessed?

James Juhnke makes the case that even though George Bush used the rhetoric of total war in the tradition of World Wars I and II, he in fact did not ask U.S. citizens to make the sacrifices (i.e., war bonds and conscription) that were required in those wars. Mennonites knew how to respond in those wars by refusing to buy war bonds and be conscripted into the military. Juhnke asks: How do Christians act faithfully in a nation with superior technology that can fight "quick" wars as the world's police force?

Several essays refer to the powerful role played by the mass media in war. What is truth in the context of war, and how do we know it? Stuart Showalter's essay unmasks the problem when he describes the mass media as "more lapdog than watchdog." We were manipulated. Do we know, for example, how much of the oil spill in the Persian Gulf was caused by coalition bombing and how much by Iraqi sabotage? The image of the pitiful water fowl struggling to get to shore out of the oil is etched firmly in our mind. As we watched this scene again and again, we were told the Iraqis had released millions of barrels of oil into the Gulf. Yet several weeks later that oil slick had not yet reached shore. So what caused the earlier oil spill? The reporters did not press the questions that needed to be asked.

North Americans did not want bad news. So when Peter Arnett did report civilian casualties in Baghdad, many accused him of aiding the enemy. A sanitized war of only collateral damage protects the facade that we are "good" people. Only the enemy is evil. We still do not know how many Iraqis were killed, probably somewhere between 100,000 and 200,000.

We know we live in a sick society when it takes a war to discover our identity. A sign of health would be a society with a common will and determination to address the fact that one in four children is born into poverty. What kinds of societies do we live in that can, in a matter of months, mobilize thousands of soldiers, send massive quantities of high-tech equipment halfway around the world, spend billions of dollars for war—yet cannot tackle problems of health care, justice for native North

Americans, homelessness, unemployment, education, drug abuse, crime, and a corroding infrastructure of streets and bridges?

Call to Faithfulness

Worthy is the Lamb who was slain, to receive power and wealth and wisdom and might and honor and glory and blessing! (Revelation 5:12)

Do not be conformed to this world but be transformed by the renewal of your mind, that you may prove what is the will of God, what is good and acceptable and perfect. (Romans 12:2)

The doxology of praise to the slain Lamb and the call to faithful obedience in the world are intimately connected. The affirmation that the slain Lamb is the Lord of history supports the conviction that the way of Jesus Christ is what endures and what is ultimately victorious. So while many celebrate a military victory, those who follow the Christ of the cross know that the real bases for an enduring peace are the fruits of the Spirit: love, joy, peace, long-suffering, gentleness, faithfulness, meekness, temperance. As James Longacre puts it in his essay: "The task of the church is to place before all the claims of the Lord of history and vision of the city 'whose builder and maker is God.' In the absence of powerful calls to the kingdom of God, people will yield to the calls and claims of lesser kingdoms."

The essays in this volume call for the mission of the church to be placed in the context of the hope we have in Jesus Christ. A military battle may have been won. However, the long-term moral and spiritual battle against the principalities and powers of darkness has a long way to go. The church's hope is based upon our foretaste of the victory over evil we have experienced in Jesus Christ.

In the light of this hope, we continue to do battle as we work.

- to develop an authentic and vital life of worship and prayer that nurtures the spirit of Christ in our lives;
- to reach out to those who are in pain, to seek justice for the poor and suffering;
- to help rebuild homes, the cities, the people's lives who have been ravaged by war;
- to become active as citizens in our own countries to help redirect our commitment to war and the instruments of war,

to pursue instead the methods of nonviolent conflict resolution;

• to build relationships of trust and understanding with, and to seek justice for, our Jewish and Muslim neighbors in the Middle East;

• to pass on to our children and young people, by example, a vision for a lifestyle of gentleness and love that is an alternative to the mass media images of selfish indulgence and violence.

It is fitting that several of the essays in this volume focus on how we pass on the faith to our children and youth. This is a special challenge, as increasingly our children and youth are bombarded by media images of triumphal violence in the defense of a way of life of materialism and self-indulgence.

Therefore, I close this introduction by highlighting Abe Bergen's essay, "Empowering Teenagers for Peacemaking." Though this volume of essays will appropriately help us reflect on the issues raised by the Persian Gulf War, Bergen says we need to go beyond intellectual discussion. Only through passionate involvement can we pass on the vision of peace to our children and youth. We are too isolated and immunized from the pain and suffering of the people of the world. Bergen suggests an action/reflection educational strategy to get youth involved. He says that "nurturing a compassionate awareness in youth begins when they become engaged in situations of injustice, when they listen to stories from victims of oppression, and when they interact with adults committed to ministries of justice and peacemaking. Such experiences impact youth on an emotional level and leave the door open for further reflection and action."

Would this not also be an appropriate educational model for adults? And must we not all begin by repenting of our sin by acknowledging the idolatry of materialism that has made us dependent upon the lifeline of oil from the Persian Gulf?

Outline of the Book

The first three chapters help us to focus especially on the theological foundations of Christian pacifism.

Chapters four through eight provide an interpretation of the Persian Gulf War within the broader flow of history, and analyze our own societies in the context of a global community.

In chapters nine through twelve, each author explores areas of conflict within our own society, proposing how we can live peaceably among neighbors with whom we disagree.

Chapters thirteen through fifteen ask how we can nurture and pass on the faith to our children and youth.

Chapter sixteen describes how five congregations responded to the Persian Gulf War.

The book concludes with an essay on spiritual resources that can sustain us in time of war.

Duane K. Friesen is professor of Bible and religion at Bethel College, North Newton, Kansas. He is author of the book Christian Peacemaking and International Conflict: A Realist Pacifist Perspective, *published in 1986 by Herald Press.*

1
What We Believe

Helmut Harder

The early leaders of the Anabaptist-Mennonite movement called upon their followers to leave war and vengeance behind and follow Jesus in the way of peace.

Uncle Jake, C.O.

Though I was only a child at the time, I remember the evening very well. We were gathered on the platform of the Vineland train station, seeing Uncle Jake off. Barely twenty, this youngest son of a large Mennonite family was on his way to Jasper National Park, some 2,500 miles to the west. It was 1941. World War II was raging, and he was headed for the mountains to plant trees rather than across the sea to fight the Germans.

As the train sounded its parting whistle, there were hurried kisses and some tears. But there were no regrets. The train received its willing passenger. Then it blew its whistle again and disappeared into the night.

Although I didn't understand everything that was going on at the time, I had heard that Uncle Jake was a C.O., a conscientious objector. And I knew he was doing a good thing. This son of the Mennonite tradition was on the right track.

Ernie Swalm, Nonresister

A year or two later, I learned another elementary lesson about war and peace from a visitor to our congregation. His name was Ernie Swalm, a bishop of the Brethren in Christ Church, a sister conference of the Mennonites. At an evening meeting in the church, he told his story. He had spent some time in the St. Catharines jail during World War I because he refused to join the Canadian army. I had seen the St. Catharines jail many times and thought it housed only criminals. But Ernie Swalm had been imprisoned there for his Christian stand against war.

My parents bought the book he had written about his experiences. It was entitled *Nonresistance Under Test*. Bishop Swalm was a nonresister. Obviously my church and my family thought that he, too, had done the right thing.

The Mennonite Tradition

The convictions of Bishop Swalm and Uncle Jake have their basis in a confessional movement that began about 400 years earlier. In 1527 a group of Anabaptists gathered at the village of Schleitheim in South Germany for what turned out to be a historic meeting. Under the guidance of Michael Sattler, they put into writing their understanding of what the earliest Anabaptists, forerunners of the Mennonites, believed.

Among other things, the Schleitheim Confession speaks against weapons and war. It reads in part as follows:

> The weapons of their [the world's] battle and warfare are carnal and only against the flesh, but the weapons of Christians are spiritual, against the fortification of the devil. The worldly are armed with steel and iron but Christians are armed with the armour of God, with truth, righteousness, peace, faith, salvation, and with the Word of God. (Howard John Loewen, *One Lord, One Church, One Hope, And One God: Mennonite Confessions of Faith*. Elkhart, Indiana: Institute of Mennonite Studies, 1985, p. 81)

The Schleitheim Confession pictures the Christian life as a battle, a spiritual battle fought with constructive weapons of truth and love.

A few years after Michael Sattler and his group wrote the Schleitheim Confession, another Anabaptist leader spoke out on the question of war and peace. His name was Menno Simons, after whom the Mennonites are named. Here is one of his poignant statements:

> All Christians are commanded to love their enemies; to do good unto those who abuse and persecute them. . . . Tell me, how can a Christian defend Scripturally retaliation, rebellion, war, striking, slaying, torturing, stealing, robbing and plundering and burning cities, and conquering countries? (John C. Wenger, *The Complete Works of Menno Simons*, p. 555)

Menno leaves no doubt about his position. War has no place in Christian faith and life.

These early leaders of the Anabaptist-Mennonite movement called upon their followers to leave war and vengeance behind and follow Jesus in the way of peace.

Holding to the Nonresistant Position

As the Mennonite church made its way into the next centuries, it continued to affirm a resolute stand against war. Two important Mennonite confessions of early Mennonite history attest to this. Here is an excerpt from the famous Dortrecht Confession of 1632:

> Regarding revenge, whereby we resist our enemies with the sword, we believe and confess that the Lord Jesus has forbidden his disciples and followers all revenge and resistance, and has thereby commanded them not to return evil for evil. . . . (Loewen, p. 68)

The Dortrecht Confession states further that it is better to flee from one country to another than to fight back when one is attacked.

This belief against war also underlies the Ris Confession, agreed to by a Mennonite gathering in Europe in 1766:

> Hence it is, as we think, self-evident that the use of deadly weapons and the carrying on of warfare to the destruction of our enemies—and even of innocent ones who have not wronged us but upon whom in war often falls the burden of misery and sorrow—is entirely unseemly for a true follower of Jesus and therefore not allowed. (Loewen, p. 100)

According to these historical confessions, war is entirely out of the question for true believers.

In taking this position, Mennonites are obviously out of step with the majority of Christians. While people generally do not like war, most Christians believe that there are so-called just wars. They would say that when a vicious aggressor attacks, it is the duty of the citizens of a country, including its Christians, to fight evildoers, even if this means killing the enemy and others who might get in the way.

Such Christians usually say that you can live in two spheres or kingdoms. In the sphere of the church you should love one another and do good. But as a faithful citizen of your country, you are duty bound to defend the nation against aggressors.

Mennonites do not follow this track. They do not divide duties in this way. How can you act in one way in the church and in another way in the world?

J. C. Wenger tells a story to illustrate the problem. The story comes from the Middle Ages:

> A peasant was strolling one Lord's Day over the land he tilled, and to his astonishment came upon his bishop who was an honorable man, but of all things the bishop was hunting rabbits.
>
> The peasant ventured to remark, "I am surprised that your excellency would go hunting on Sunday."
>
> "I am not hunting as a bishop," was the reply: "I am hunting as a prince."
>
> The peasant scratched his head and answered, "If the devil gets the prince, what will happen to the bishop?" (*The Way of Peace*, Scottdale: Herald Press, 1977, pp. 58f.)

Mennonites believe that it is never right to kill, not on Sunday nor during the week; not in the church nor in the world; not among friends nor among enemies.

At times governments have allowed those who will not fight for conscience' sake to do alternate service, like Uncle Jake did. At other times ruling authorities have not allowed such privileges. In such cases conscientious objectors have refused to join the military. Like Ernie Swalm, some have been imprisoned for their faithful stand. A Mennonite confession of 1933 supports this direction:

> We believe that a Christian's duty is to be subject to the higher powers, but when demands are made contrary to our convictions from the Word of God, e.g., military service, we

are governed by the word of the apostles: "We ought to obey God rather than man." (Loewen, p. 111)

It was this conviction that motivated Uncle Jake to take the road less traveled, and that led Ernie Swalm to sit resolutely among the lawbreakers in a county jail.

It must be said that not all young men from Mennonite communities took this stand. In the European Mennonite community, many joined the armies of their countries. In North America as well, a significant number of young men of Mennonite background complied with the draft during wars of the twentieth century. But this was done contrary to what Mennonites have maintained in their confessions.

The 1950 Shift

During the centuries before World War II, it was typical of Mennonites to remain quiet and neutral in the country of their citizenship. They hoped the government would leave them to their daily tasks and their church life. They wanted to preserve what they believed, and, if possible, to keep their own communities free of involvement in the military. They wanted to be left to themselves.

But by the end of World War II there was a change in direction. This became evident at an important gathering of sixty-five Mennonite leaders in 1950. The Winona Lake Study Conference on Nonresistance was set up to reflect on how the Mennonite church had responded to the two devastating wars of the first half of the century and to set a course for the future.

The study conference resulted in a statement called the "Declaration of Christian Faith and Commitment" (pamphlet published by Peace Section, Mennonite Central Committee, Akron, Pennsylvania). The statement reveals a broadening vision of the Mennointe peace witness. While in the past Mennonites had kept their views on war and peace for themselves, the statement speaks of love and peace as the heritage of all people, a way "to which all . . . are called" (Section II). This means that the church must witness "of the righteousness which God requires of all men, even in government" (Section III).

As mentioned above, in the past, Mennonites thought mainly of themselves when they spoke of peace. In this statement the church is defined as a "universal community . . . which must go out into all human society" (Section II). And the peace witness is not simply something to be preserved for Mennonites; it should permeate "all human relations, both individual and social" (Section II).

Further, the declaration spoke not only of nonresistance in times of conflict, but also of noncooperation with the military in the broadest sense. Mennonites want no part in

> financing war operations or preparations through war bonds . . . participation in the manufacture of munitions, weapons, and instruments of war and destruction . . . in scientific, educational, or cultural programs designed to contribute to war, or in any propaganda or activity that tends to promote ill-will or hatred among men or nations. (Section III)

Finally, on war itself, the leaders gathered at Winona Lake took a bold new stance, claiming that Mennonites were ready to get directly involved in constructive ways:

> If war does come with its possible serious devastation from bombings or other forms of destruction, such as atomic blasts, germ warfare, poison gas, etc., we will willingly render every help which conscience permits, sacrificially and without thought of personal safety, so long as we thereby help to preserve and restore life and not to destroy it. (Section III)

Without doubt, the "Declaration on Christian Faith and Commitment" brought a new vision to the peace witness of Mennonites in North America.

This broadened vision of peace can be found in Mennonite confessions of faith in the decades that followed. The Mennonite Church Confession of 1963 states: "We must aggressively, at the risk of life itself, do whatever we can for the alleviation of human distress and suffering" (Loewen, p. 77). A Mennonite Brethren Confession of 1975 says: "The Christian seeks to practice Christ's law of love in all situations, including those involving personal injustice, social upheaval and international tensions" (Loewen, p. 178). Clearly, Mennonites have moved from an attitude of nonresistant self-preservation to a stance of creative involvement in peacemaking.

But the Mennonite belief stated at Winona Lake—that war is wrong for everyone, not just for Mennonites—still needs to be proclaimed. And forty years after the Winona Lake study conference, Mennonites are making the point in a renewed way. The recent publication in which Mennonites also participated, *A Declaration on Peace* (Scottdale: Herald Press, 1990, p. 11), insists that loyalty to a faithful understanding and commitment to Jesus Christ is not compatible with participation in war. The declaration is addressed to "all who claim to be Christian" (p. 9).

Issues That Persist

In the second half of the twentieth century, Mennonites have continued to ponder certain issues related to warfare. First, there is the question of how to regard the wars of the Old Testament. Mennonite confessions of faith clearly point to Jesus Christ as the one who settled this question with the words: "You have heard that it was said, 'An eye for an eye and a tooth for a tooth. . . .' But I say to you, Love your enemies and pray for those who persecute you" (Matthew 5:38, 44).

This emphasis on Jesus as one who supersedes the Old Testament is also seen in the words of Peter to Cornelius, "You know the message he sent to the people of Israel, preaching peace by Jesus Christ—he is Lord of all" (Acts 10:36). It is also instructive to center nonviolence in the atonement of Christ. Since Jesus died "once for all" (1 Peter 3:18), Christians should preach forgiveness rather than punishment and death for wrongdoing. Notwithstanding these perspectives, Mennonites keep raising the question about how to understand the Old Testament wars.

A second question concerns the payment of taxes which support war. Is there any real difference between going to war or paying so that others may go to war? Many people have a bad conscience about paying for war through taxes. The Bible does say that we should pay the government its due (Mark 12:13-17; Romans 13:1-10), and obey the government (Romans 13:1ff.). Yet we cannot believe that the Bible wants to encourage believers to assist in killing. This has led some Mennonites to withhold that portion of taxes which supports the military.

Studies that have been done on this question have yielded two major conclusions. First, we should support those persons who, for conscience' sake, wish to withhold payment of taxes which contribute to war. Second, we are encouraged to support the Peace Tax Fund.

Third, can Mennonites engage in public acts to demonstrate their opposition to war? Recently some have shown their displeasure with the war machine by attending prayer vigils at missile sites and writing letters imploring their governments to stop fighting. Recently a delegation of Mennonites went to Baghdad to speak about peace with the Iraqis. Beyond these efforts, some Mennonites have engaged in symbolic acts of protest, such as breaking the law by crossing into restricted areas where weapons are manufactured.

There is a continuing debate on the practice of civil disobedience. Some argue for it, comparing it to prophetic acts of the Old Testament. Others are against actions which break the laws of the country. In the meantime, the Christian Peacemaker Team movement, an initiative originating at the Mennonite World Conference of 1983 and endorsed by some Mennonite churches, is helping Mennonite peace activists to channel their energies in helpful directions.

In Conclusion: On Track?

During the recent war in the Persian Gulf, individuals and groups in Mennonite churches actively and resolutely spoke against the war. Congregations drafted letters; conference groups issued statements; the Mennonite Central Committee addressed its own constituency as well as governments. Mennonites organized prayer vigils and joined groups gathering in strategic places to make their witness known. Letters were addressed to Rev. Billy Graham, criticizing his seeming support of President Bush's decision on January 15 to attack Iraq.

However, this story has another side. A significant number of Mennonite individuals, along with the majority of citizens in Canada and the United States, spoke in favor of the attack on Iraq. Our study of what Mennonites believe about war should make it clear that, in doing so, they broke faith with the historic, biblical understanding that the Mennonite church has held throughout the centuries.

Personally, I'm on track with Menno Simons, with Ernie Swalm, with Uncle Jake, and with Jesus Christ, the Prince of Peace and the Lord of glory.

Helmut Harder, on leave from his position as professor of theology at Canadian Mennonite Bible College, Winnipeg, Manitoba, is serving as general secretary for the Conference of Mennonites in Canada.

2
Pacifism and Patriotism

James Longacre

As passions swell in times of war, the room for question, reflection, and perspective diminishes. . . . To suggest that there might have been another way is seen as siding with the enemy.

Wars, particularly popular wars, put the Christian pacifist on the defensive. When the band plays the national anthem and the crowds sing with enthusiasm and conviction, the pacifist struggles. As neighbors display the flags in support of war, the pacifist not wishing to be unpatriotic by definition, wonders what to do. As the sons and daughters of neighbors leave the community for military duty, no one wishes to question their commitment and dedication to a cause.

As passions swell in times of war, the room for question, reflection, and perspective diminishes. The enemy is characterized as evil. The national cause is listed as necessary and right. To probe, to question, is received by others as undercutting, weakening the national effort. To suggest that there might have been another way is seen as siding with the enemy.

Whereas in normal times pacifist Christians are viewed by others as holding an interesting position, in times of war pacifism stirs anger, hostility, condemnation. In times of peace pacifists are tolerated, even respected by some, but in times of war pacifists are called cowards, and accused of unwillingness to defend the freedoms they cherish.

So how should the Christian pacifist live and speak in the midst of patriotic fervor? Shall we simply hunker down until the patriotic emotion passes? Shall we find ways to be a little patriotic—fly small flags, for example? Shall we go to great lengths to demonstrate our respect for government and our appreciation and gratefulness for the freedoms we have and argue that it is only on this one small matter, namely pacifism, that we are a little different?

I would suggest that, in the midst of patriotic fervor, we choose not to be arrogant, nor defiant, nor defensive. Let us rather, quietly and persistently, do what as Christians we are called to be and do. In the times of patriotic fervor in the midst of war (and in times of peace) let us: 1) affirm the primacy of the kingdom; 2) love the neighbor; and 3) sing the songs of Zion.

The Primacy of the Kingdom

Christians, like others, live in the midst of many claims, many demands, many authorities. There are the claims of family, job, church, community, the bank loan, and more. Sorting through these many claims becomes, at times, a juggling act of no little skill.

For many people, the nation stands quite high in the listing of the authorities laying claim to their lives. Surely delight in one's country, respect for governmental authorities, appreciation for individual and religious freedoms are not faults. But how much deference, loyalty, and allegiance should the Christian give the nation? At what points might the claims of the nation trespass upon the call and claims of God? How does the Christian hold these in appropriate proportion?

The Scriptures are not silent on these matters. Jesus put it directly on several occasions. His followers are to seek the kingdom first. Even the texts that lay out the claims of governing authorities hold these claims to some limits.

When Jesus was asked to address the issue of payment of taxes to Caesar, his answer clearly placed limits on what was Caesar's. To render to Caesar what is Caesar's and to God what is God's suggests each has a claim, but it hardly suggests that these claims are equal.

The text from Romans 13, which is the clearest New Testament recognition of governing authorities, nevertheless proposes limits. While Christians are enjoined to provide what is due—taxes, revenue, respect, and honor—Christians are to provide only what is due, not more.

The point is made even more directly in 1 Peter 2:13 which reads: "Honor everyone. Love the family of believers. Fear God. Honor the emperor." No one dare suggest that the measure of commitment, dedication, worship, awe which we offer to God is similarly due the emperor.

In the midst of patriotic fervor, this sense of what is due God and what is due the nation tends again and again to get confused and out of proportion. Nations seek to put forward claims that press into that which belongs to God. In times of war, particularly, the calls for patriotism, loyalty to the nation exceeds that which is due.

Historians call this heightened sense of loyalty and patriotism, nationalism. In various cultures, amid differing religions, nationalism in recent centuries has taken on clear religious dimensions. James E. Wood, Jr., wrote: "Twentieth-century nationalism has all the earmarks of a religion." Wood adds that "nationalism today, whenever found, has its requirements of worship and ritual, its possessions, its pilgrimages, its holy days, its temples, its shrines, its prophets of the past, its mythology, and its gospel of faith. Its essential doctrine, simply stated, is the exaltation of the state to supreme authority and the demand of a loyalty which supercedes all other loyalties" ("The Problem of Nationalism in Church-State Relationships," *Journal of Church and State*, Spring 1968, p. 259).

Undoubtedly, people will worship. Loyalty will be given to something. Most yearn for a cause larger than themselves. The task of the church is to place before all the claims of the Lord of history and the vision of the city "whose builder and maker is God." In the absence of powerful calls to the kingdom of God, people will yield to the calls and claims of lesser kingdoms.

Love the Neighbor

As the sons and daughters of our neighbors sign on with the military, pacifists are often asked how we, as Christian pacifists, serve the nation. What do we offer? In times of war the issue is even more pressing. As others find themselves in harm's way (as the military puts it) in defense of the national interests, what do we sacrifice?

We can easily feel guilty, negligent, defensive. We need not.

Surely the call of Christ and the call of the church, to acts of compassion and deeds of mercy, if obeyed, offer a needed and enduring contribution to the nation and beyond. To feed the hungry, to labor for justice, to provide housing for the poor, this serves the nation.

Thus, let one and all in our communities of faith continue to heed Christ's call. Let there continue to be strong involvement in voluntary service, in Mennonite Disaster Service work, in Mennonite Central Committee assignments, in local volunteer organizations, and more.

In the community in which I live and work, Mennonites carry a disproportionate share of responsibility in caring for the elderly, in working with the developmentally disabled, in ministry with the mentally ill. That is as it should be.

How do Christian pacifists make their contribution? By concern for those near and far who need care and love.

Sing the Songs of Zion

In actual practice the separation of church and state in the United States, perhaps Canada as well, is not as clear as the constitutional prescriptions. Perhaps it need not be. Surely perspectives of the Christian faith should address all aspects of life including the economic, social, and political. Some suggest that a society needs the transcendent values of religions within which the claims and expectations of the civil order find reference.

However, the uncritical fusion of religion and patriotism, most in evidence at times of war, is an unholy brew and a potent one. The courtship and marriage of God and country serves neither the nation or the church well.

Nations, undoubtedly—perhaps understandably—act in self-interest in the search for power and the need for economic well-being. Nations should be seen for what they are—flawed instruments and often very selfish. Presidential prayer breakfasts and the frequent invoking of "God Bless America" or other pious expressions of political leaders rarely transform the actual policies and direction of the nation.

The use of moral and religious language to describe the intent and direction of national policy hardly makes it moral and good. A president's declaration that our cause is just and right may well conceal the truth. The characterization of the enemy as evil moves war into a moral campaign rather than holding wars to a stated redress of a grievance.

A God-and-country mix tends to give greater legitimacy to the nation than the biblical perspective would warrant. Loyalty and allegiance that belongs singularly to God is corralled by the nation. By pious language, national self-interest and even acts of injustice and oppression are reclothed and declared right.

A God-and-country mix is bad for the church. Beliefs and understandings of the Christian faith are violated. Let me list several.

First, in a God-and-country mix, the understanding that God is God of all the earth is compromised. The prayer and plea for God to bless a nation's military endeavors seeks to bring God onto our side. It seeks to provide legitimacy for our nation's efforts. John Howard Yoder stated that no government should claim to speak for God. No nation should presume God's aid for selfish pursuits (*The Priestly Kingdom*, Notre Dame, Indiana: University of Notre Dame Press, 1984, p. 189).

Secondly, a God-and-country mix seriously jeopardizes the Christian's understanding of, and commitment to, the body of Christ around the world. As members of this community of faith drawn from tribes and peoples and nations, we confess that these are our brothers and sisters in Christ. It is this people, this "holy nation," that holds our fervent love and care (See Chapter 4, "The Universal Church" in John M. Drescher, *Why I Am a Conscientious Objector*, Scottdale, Pennsylvania: Herald Press, 1982, pp. 43-48).

Thirdly, the God-and-country mix neglects profound biblical themes. In the pious public prayers for the nation, where are the themes of sin, judgment, and repentance? One only hears blessing and benediction, but no prophetic critique. Whereas most Christians can find evidences of sin nearly everywhere, somehow the nation is exempt.

Finally, the God of whom the Scriptures give witness, the God whom we have come to know in Jesus of Nazareth, is a God who loves the enemy. There is something fully and blatantly contradictory in invoking the blessing of this God who loves the enemy while the nation deliberately sets out to destroy the enemy.

The purposes of the nation and the church would be served best if the patriotic hymns were reserved for the national holidays and the songs of Zion were reserved for the church's Sabbath and holy days. Let the flags fly at the public buildings. The church has its own marvelous symbols—bread and cup, cross and dove, and holy hands embracing one and all.

For the Christian pacifist, the central issue is neither patriotism or unpatriotism. The central matter is to be faithful to the call of the Lord. In response to that call, the Christian pacifist seeks first the kingdom, loves the neighbor, and sings the songs of Zion.

James Longacre, Barto, Pennsylvania, serves as coordinator for the Franconia Mennonite Conference. A graduate of Eastern Mennonite College and Baylor University, he was a pastor for more than seventeen years.

3
War's Impact on the Poor

Hubert Brown

Nations that value life and cherish human beings can find ways to share their resources. . . . War is a handy diversion from the failure of a nation to deal with pressing domestic issues.

The way of peace they know not, and there is no justice in their paths; they have made their roads crooked, no one who goes in them knows peace. (Isaiah 59:8)

During the U.S. Civil War, General Sherman said, "War is hell." Indeed, war is hell, a horrible hell. The hell is not just for those who are engaged in combat, but for many other people as well.

The consequences of modern-day war extend far beyond the massive destruction by the weapons used. The costs are far greater than what we can ever imagine. They arise both from the dangers from the weapons used, and from the economic, social, political, and environmental damage that the weapons help to create. These costs are often indirect and harder to see, but they reach deep into our society. On the whole these costs have been as destructive as battlefield warfare itself. This essay will deepen our understanding of the costs of war in our society and in our world. We must acknowledge not only the risk of future destruction, but also the cost of the war in the Persian Gulf.

I write as a Christian. I write as one who has committed my life to Jesus Christ as Savior and Lord. In Jesus Christ I've discovered the everlasting, merciful God, who is reconciling the world into one. Through Jesus Christ humanity can be saved. Through Jesus Christ humanity can experience peace.

The peace of God is all-embracing. Nothing can separate us from it—neither life nor death, neither political powers nor earthly authorities. God's peace transcends all understanding, and it is available to enlighten, guide, and direct the paths humans tread. God's peace means not having to respond to the other in violence. God's peace means not having to resolve conflicts and antagonisms with weapons of war. God's peace encompasses God's love.

God's peace is also a call to believers—a call to a radical obedience to Jesus Christ as Lord. As a believer, I stand with others who are bound to Jesus Christ as disciples. Ours is a call to discipleship. The call to discipleship is a call to the community of Jesus Christ. In the community of Jesus Christ all life is sacred, and our calling is to affirm life.

Our calling is to spread the teachings of Jesus Christ. We are to be peacemakers, as Jesus Christ indicated in his Sermon on the Mount. We are called to reject those understandings and teachings that would limit the Sermon on the Mount to a privatized religion, and thus remove it from social and political responsibility here on earth.

Discipleship and following in the steps of Jesus Christ take place in the midst of community. This commitment involves one's whole heart, soul, and strength.

The Gospel of Peace

The conscience of believers is determined by the gospel of peace. Through Christ we have found peace with God. We now identify with Jesus Christ. Our identity and moral integrity is in Christ. We cannot act against our conscience without renouncing our identity. We therefore will act on our conscience and endorse and support all that is consistent with our understanding of Jesus Christ, who is our Lord.

I am, therefore, as a Christian, a peacemaker and a pacifist. As a pacifist, I am a conscientious objector to the taking of human life. Charles A. Maresca, Jr., associate director of the National Interreligious Service Board for Conscientious Objectors, stated what we as Christian pacifists and conscientious objectors believe. He is quoted on a poster as saying:

So, for the record, here is what conscientious objectors object to: We object to killing. We object to killing in the name of capitalism, we object to killing in the name of communism, we object to killing in the name of religion. We object to being forced to register for war and killing, we object to being forced to participate in the preparations for war and killing. We object to killing innocent civilians, and we object to killing soldiers. We object to nuclear weapons, we object to conventional weapons. When war comes, many of us will perform peaceful alternative service. Many of us will go to jail rather than compromise our deeply held beliefs. But we will not fight. We will not kill.

The biblical mandate for God's children, Christians, is declared in the one word, *shalom*. Shalom means peace. This peacemaking task demands a great deal from us. It calls us to listen to the cries of the poor and the oppressed. It calls us to hear the message of the powerless. It calls us to act by God's power to do whatever we can do to break down the walls of hostility that separate people from God and from others, and to heal the needs and hurts of our world.

For people of faith, any critique of society is in a real sense measured against the biblical concept of shalom, that is, the overall economic and spiritual health of humanity in relationship to the whole of creation. No definition of peace, or shalom, can ignore social injustice. As Christians, we believe that the strength and security of a nation is measured by how that nation treats the poor and homeless and weak.

Times of war are never easy times in which to be a pacifist. Times of war are not the easiest times to challenge the whole of society to reorder priorities and to work at solving domestic problems. It's easy to write about war while one's nation is at peace. To write about opposition to war while one's nation is engaged in bomb dropping and missile attacks is much more difficult. To write about war as being horrible, wrong, immoral, and unjust while a war is going on, is to risk receiving scorn, rejection, and even outright hatred from many people.

This certainly is true in North America. Nonetheless, as a Christian, I still believe that war is wrong. The fact that a war was taking place as I write does not change my opposition to war. Recently I was involved in a peace vigil with others from my community. A large delegation of pro-war, pro-troop people came and surrounded us. And they said "all manner of evil against us" for our public witness for peace. Nothing is easier than accusing those who oppose war as unpatriotic. Whenever this nation goes to war those who voice their conscientious objection to killing are labeled unpatriotic. In my community, one man had a big sign stating that we were "stabbing our troops in the back." Those who support war, and the Persian Gulf War in particular, accuse others of opposing not the war, but the brave men and women in uniform sent to fight and die in it.

I want to make it clear that as a Christian I am opposed to all wars—those fought by middle-class reservists, men and women, those fought by poor minorities, those fought by poor whites, those fought by Arabs, and those fought by the West, and those fought by people anywhere.

A friend of mine had a T-shirt that said, "Join the Army, see interesting places, meet new people, and kill them." The equal opportunity to kill and to die does not appeal to me. It is not appealing as the new world order. Nor does it appeal as the promise for a bright new future. It does not appeal to me as being a kinder and gentler way to be.

Nations that value life and cherish human beings can find ways to share their resources. Citizens can have adequate health care, accessible education, an end to homelessness and pain. This is the kind of nation that I think of as kind and gentle.

Turning Away from Society's Pain

Whether by design or not, war is a handy diversion from the failure of a nation to deal with pressing domestic issues. Are we trying to simply forget and not think about our failing banks, our education crisis, our drug crisis, poor health care, rampant crime problems, runaway unemployment, racism, sexism, corruption, and all of the other problems that threaten our society? We cannot simply say, "Have a nice day," and fail to address every aspect of those things that are deteriorating. We cannot worship a homeless Man on Sundays and ignore homeless women and men on Monday.

Dwight D. Eisenhower said, "Every gun that is made, every warship launched, every rocket fired signifies, in the final sense, a theft from those who hunger and are not fed, those who are cold and not clothed." The Persian Gulf War, as all wars, was a theft. It was a theft to those who are poverty-stricken, to those who suffer from hunger and malnutrition, those who are homeless and helpless.

The United States and Canada are the richest, most fortunate nations in the history of the world. Yet millions of people in our midst do not share in the abundance and wealth. A theft has taken place. Millions in our midst have not been granted the comforts and opportunities they see all around them. They are poor. The poor are trapped. They have few choices.

I know what it's like to be poor. I grew up in eastern Pennsylvania in a dark and dingy house. I can still see the falling wallpaper, the cracked plaster, the grubby floor, the broken window panes. I can see us huddled around an old wood stove in the kitchen to keep warm. I remember the lack of food in the cupboards, the rags used as mattresses for beds, the hand-me-down clothes, and the desire to eat.

To be poor means not having economic resources. To be poor means not having money or food. To be poor means not living decently. Being poor includes run-down homes, dirty streets, crowded apartments, limited play areas, the stench of garbage, poor schools, malnutrition, and being at the bottom of income distribution.

I remember the degrading conditions of my past. To be poor is to wear cheap clothes. Being poor means living in miserable homes. Today it sometimes means having no home at all. To be poor means having food of bad quality or none at all. Being poor means ill health caused by an unbalanced diet. To be poor means to live from handout to handout. Being poor becomes a way of life. Poverty robs one of one's dignity. Poverty saps you of your potential. Poverty makes it impossible for you to share what the North American way of life is supposed to be.

Profile of a Poor Person

Who are the poor? They are invisible North Americans. They are in our midst, like Lazarus at the gate, but we do not see them. They are folk who cannot find employment. They are folk who cannot meet their reasonable needs. They are folk who are physically and mentally disabled who, as a result, can't find jobs. They are old folks and young folks. They are the uneducated, the unskilled, the dropouts. They are largely the racial minorities—Blacks, Puerto Ricans, Native people, Haitians, boat people, and undocumented refugees.

Here is a poor person profile: You are nonwhite. You belong to a family of no wage earners headed by a female. Your family has more than six kids, all under eighteen. You're between the ages of fourteen and twenty-five, or over sixty-five. You live in a ghetto or barrio or on a reservation. You have fewer than eight years of education.

The poor have access to fewer educational and economic opportunities. They are discriminated against. The poor often receive low-quality health care. They are often malnourished. The poor are more likely to be victims of crimes against the person (armed robbery, assault, murder). The poor are also more likely to be victimized by property crimes (break-ins). The poor are often given harsher treatment by law enforcement officials. They have less political clout. The poor are a minority. They cannot contribute large sums of money to campaign funds. They do not tend to run candidates. They sometimes have low voter participation. Their already weak political position is often further undercut by job and welfare injustice against those who vote, by gerrymandering of election districts, and by the emphasis on electing officials at-large rather than from a specific district. The poor have less influence on the job and within the community. Many are dependent on public assistance. The poor are vulnerable to family dysfunction and breakdown.

The poor in America number around forty million. About three million people in the United States are homeless, about a third of them entire families. One out of five children in the United States lives in poverty. Millions are unemployed and underemployed and have no prospects in sight for real work. These statistics are disturbing, and if something isn't done, we risk writing off an entire generation of people from leading productive lives.

I am a Black and my people, Black America, are most directly affected by rampant poverty. Another Black American, Jesse Jackson, said,

> The economic, political, and social state of black America is not new. Its state or condition has only been intensified. Black America is in an intensified state of brokenness, misery, and despair....
> Black America is being victimized by a cutback in schools and an increase in jails; a cutback in food stamps and an increase in hunger and malnutrition; a cutback in affirmative

action and an increase in unemployment; a cutback in health care and an increase in infant mortality; a cutback in housing and an increase in home foreclosures and in people living in their cars; a cutback in legal enforcement and an increase in racial discrimination.

We are used for scapegoats—as the cause of the nation's misery—and we are the objects of violent attacks by the KKK, the Nazis, the police, and the government—sometimes they are one and the same. (*BEYOND OPPORTUNITY: Jesse Jackson's vision for America,* by Roger D. Hatch, Fortress Press, 1988, pp. 33-34)

As I look over the landscape of North America I see pain, brokenness, unemployment, poverty, and helplessness also among whites, Indians, farmers, women, children, refugees, and many others. Poverty has no hold on one group over the other. Our nations turn their backs on all who are poor, helpless, vulnerable, and needy.

More Weapons Mean Less Bread

American and Canadian military policies, and certainly the Persian Gulf War, represent a theft from the poor. Military expenditures are directly linked to the suffering of the poor, particularly in the United States. In order to pay for the ever burgeoning military and war-making powers, resources have been sapped that could have gone to change the conditions of the poor. This problem is guns versus butter, or bread versus bombs. The budget maneuvers of the 1980s and 1990s have structured and fashioned the federal budget in such a way that increased military spending has taken place at the expense of the poor.

Over the last decade in the United States we have witnessed billions of dollars lost to needed domestic programs. The Pentagon's military buildup has been paid for by cuts in social programs aimed at helping the poor. The military buildup and the war has meant the loss of $41 billion for health care, $29 billion in education, $14 billion in food, $7 billion in low-income housing, and $14 billion for natural resources and environment. Every military buildup is financed by cuts in social programs.

William Sloane Coffin, president of SANE/FREEZE, made headlines recently when he stated,

The cost of these weapons makes them a justice issue. . . . For one trillion dollars, you could build a $75,000 house, place it on $5,000 worth of land, furnish it with $10,000 worth of furniture, put a $10,000 car in the garage—and give all this to each and every family in Kansas, Missouri, Nebraska, Oklahoma, Colorado, and Utah. Having done this, you would still have enough money to build 500 schools at $10 million each for the communities in the region. And after that, you would still have enough left out of the original trillion to put aside, at 10 percent annual interest, a sum of money that would pay a salary of $25,000 per year for an army of 10,000 nurses, the same salary for an army of 10,000 teachers, and an annual cash allowance of $5,000 for each and every family throughout the six-state region—not just for one year, but forever. . . . And that is only one-half of what President Reagan has spent on military weaponry alone. . . . And while we may be number one in global military bases and naval fleets, in nuclear bombs and warheads, we are presently number five in literacy rate, eight in life expectancy, 14 in available safe water, 18 in infant mortality rate, and 20 in school-age population per teacher. (*Nuclear Times*, May/June 1988)

Now is the time to cry out for change. We need to cry out in sanity and goodwill. People are dying. Children are being destroyed. Homelessness, hunger, poverty, racism, and drug abuse stalk our land. Funds for war and other military projects are needlessly hurting poor communities. Each night millions of North Americans feel powerless and insecure because of unmet basic human needs. The tragedy is the careless squandering of money to fund new and improved ways to kill while critical domestic needs go disregarded. Money for more weapons guarantees that the poor will not have food, jobs, and a place to live.

The church has a prophetic task: to denounce the structures of injustice which promote and sustain militarism and war. The church is called to help create a new vision for North America that provides for the needs of hurting people. This is the task of peacemaking, reconciliation, and agape love.

Hubert Brown serves as executive secretary for the General Conference Mennonite Church's Commission on Home Ministries. Previously he served as pastor of Calvary Mennonite Church and as superintendent of Calvary Christian School, both in Inglewood, California. He has studied at Goshen Biblical Seminary and holds a doctorate from California Graduate School of Theology.

4
Where Will War Lead Us?

George Dyck

If all our energy goes into planning and fighting wars, we cannot survive, either because our food gathering suffers or because we finally become the victims instead of the victors.

The Origin of War

Of all the creatures on this earth, the human species is the only one that conducts wars. Animals are certainly capable of killing, but in most cases the killing is aimed at another kind of animal, and mostly to defend territory or to seek food.

Humans have a rather unique history of engaging in large-scale organized contests among themselves in which the aim is to kill members of the opposing group rather than to just subdue or to expel. Among the great apes, individual contests in which the aim is to establish a hierarchy of control are common, but rarely does one see a fight to the death such as is characteristic of warfare among humans.

The questions this human uniqueness raises are worth pondering, because they strike at the heart of the nature of humankind. Does our ability to reason inevitably lead us to the conclusion that war is the best policy for survival? Does our capacity to think cause us to believe that we are best served by killing our enemy before the enemy kills us? Is it only the less intellectually developed creatures that seek to stay out of harm's way rather than to destroy that which is perceived as a threat?

Most of us do not want to believe this interpretation about the human race's violent tendencies. We have, after all, been taught that killing is bad under most circumstances. The religions of the world all teach respect for other persons, again under *most* circumstances. Yet again and again we find our kind invoking those exceptional circumstances in which we can rationalize that it is appropriate to wage war.

Therefore, it is necessary to look at what it is about us that causes us to fight wars, rather than to pretend we are fighting "a war to end all wars," or to "secure the peace." Such slogans have been invoked with ever more force as we seek to hide the fact that we want to kill the enemy because we see it as the best means of furthering our own ends. Our motives usually are to protect or enhance our wealth, security, and freedom.

On the matter of protecting ourselves, it is a common experience for us to feel threatened by those whom we do not understand. We are far more likely to see our interests threatened than notice that we are threatening another's interests. In the Middle East, for example, we keenly perceive the threat to our energy independence because we have felt the past effect of oil embargoes. For Arabs in that region of the world it is hard to understand why we should feel threatened by these actions, because they believe what they have done has been for legitimate defensive reasons, and only raised prices to the level they thought they should have been in any case. Even in the case of a complete embargo, we would still have been more privileged than most people living in Africa, Asia, or even the Middle East.

The differences in perception of the have's and the have not's is a clear example of how wars arise between peoples of differing wealth. Those who have greater wealth or privilege readily become accustomed to it and see any challenge to their advantage as a threat which must be fended off, if necessary by force. Those of lesser wealth or privilege may believe they have a legitimate cause which must be advanced, even if it means shedding blood.

The human race gained its advantage in the world by using foresight and cunning to subdue creatures of vastly superior speed and strength. No creature on this earth has not been challenged by Homo sapiens. We showed little mercy as we subdued the earth. We have given no quarter except to those creatures which consented to be used by us for our purposes.

The lessons we learned in the war of the species, the tactics we developed and which worked so well for us there, we have been tempted to turn upon our own kind. The story of Cain and Abel suggests as much. Cain, the successful hunter, turned upon Abel because Cain both suspected him and coveted what he had.

Peace Versus War in History

If war has been so successful in our past, why all the talk of peace? Why all the effort to disguise war as peacekeeping? Clearly, too much war is counterproductive. If all our energy goes into planning and fighting wars, we cannot survive, either because our food gathering suffers or because we finally become the victims instead of the victors. Animals might be subdued to the point where they can never pose a serious threat to our collective survival. But other human beings, who can think and plan as we can, may eventually be able to defeat us if the fighting is intense enough. Societies which have been too warlike have spent themselves in wars, so that they no longer posed a serious threat to other more peaceful societies. But equally true is the observation that peaceful societies which were unable to defend themselves were destroyed by warlike peoples who did not pay much heed to the values of what may have been superior civilizations. Sometimes these conquered civilizations were able to win over their rulers to more humane and orderly ways. Such was the case for many centuries in China, as successive waves of nomadic conquerors took over an ancient civilization only to be at least partially molded by it. But at other times, peaceful societies were wiped out by invaders who had less appreciation for peace and less respect for human life.

The rise of traditions and religious beliefs helped stabilize relationships between clans and tribes. Rules and understanding about when to go to war and when to live in peace made it possible to feel more secure.

But still there were those times when traditions conflicted and relationships between peoples reached an impasse. Each party was afraid of being annihilated by surprise attack. The logical way of dealing with the anxiety created by the hostility was to plan a first strike, thereby gaining freedom from constant fear and danger.

The confidence brought about by the process of preparing and gaining the advantage of surprise was so inviting that it frequently overrode the taboos against war. Such taboos may have arisen as wise leaders found ways to make peace through treaties which were advantageous to both parties. But sometimes the latent impulses, which served so well in the battles against animals, won out and another cycle of violence was initiated, all but obliterating the gains made by earlier stages.

The story of the children of Israel gives us an insight into forces of war and peace that existed in the minds of the people who believed they were the chosen of God. Their God was ruler of not only their small corner of the earth, but of all the universe. At times they felt called of God to annihilate the enemy, as was the case when they entered the Promised Land. At other times they subdued their enemies and made them servants. On still other occasions they sought to live side by side in peace with another nation.

Jonah's story is clear testimony to the value of living in harmony with another nation, instead of destroying it. Jonah teaches us to search our motives in preaching repentance. It seems a remarkable coincidence that we face the same question again in our time—to preach repentance to the people of Nineveh or to destroy it. We have chosen the option which Jonah abandoned after getting his lesson in the belly of a whale! It is as though we want to show Jonah what it would have been like had he been able to defy God and have his own way. The recent war is a sinister reminder that in the centuries that have passed since then, we have not moved to a more peaceful way of dealing with conflict. Just the opposite.

Jesus brought a more inclusive interpretation to the concept of the people of God, and his disciples put it into action by witnessing without regard to racial or ethnic origin.

But in the centuries since Jesus' time, those who would not accept the lordship of Christ have often been aggressively destroyed. The Christian Crusaders who entered Jerusalem killed Jews and Moslems with complete abandon. It was as though all the teachings of Jesus about loving one's enemy and about the peacemakers being blessed were incomprehensible to those who called upon his name. The world seemed quite unready for this way of living. Living in peace was synonymous with the complete withdrawal from society practiced by some monastic orders.

Beginning in about the sixteenth century, the long-established European order was challenged. New ways of thinking appeared and overturned previously unquestioned religious precepts.

This opened the door to questioning many other fixed beliefs. Some people were optimistic that the new age of reason could eliminate war as soon as enough people realized there were better ways of solving conflicts. Humanistic and democratic ideas gained ground and were proposed as the basis for a new world order. World War I created profound disillusionment as frightful numbers were killed in trench warfare. The use of chemical agents to kill large numbers of combatants heightened the horror. Even enlightened, reasoning people were capable of sinking rather quickly to a level of brutality as deep as history had ever seen.

The New Meaning of War

The new element in the picture in the twentieth century was the increasing efficiency with which mass killing could be carried out. New technology not only made it easier to kill, it created a distance between the killer and the victim. The act of killing became less impassioned and, consequently, easier. Instead of finding a way to substitute negotiation for killing, reason served to justify war as "defense," or any one of countless other euphemisms. The scale of killing during World War II was the most massive ever seen. But it was not until near the end of that war, when the first nuclear bombs were exploded, that it became apparent that whole civilizations could now be destroyed overnight. War had taken on new meaning.

When the threat of annihilation of human life in whole regions, continents, perhaps the whole world, became a reality, war was no longer a way for one tribe or nation to gain dominance over another. War became the way for all of humankind to exit the world scene as countless species had done before, except that the human species would do it in its own unique way, bringing about its own destruction. John had pictured it in the book of Revelation. Human reason foresaw it in the reading of history which noted that, once invented, weapons of war are always eventually used to the fullest extent possible. But is it really to be that way?

The human psyche has developed some peculiar mental mechanisms which have accompanied the rise of consciousness. Because it is sometimes too painful to see ourselves as we are, we have had to develop disguises. Cain would have been destroyed had he been forced to fully face up to his crime. The Genesis account has him saying, "My punishment is heavier than I can bear." From a psychological viewpoint we can say that he was spared the full consequences of his act. Denial and rationalization helped minimize the evil, and Cain went on to live his life, forgetting the past as well as he was able to. So we all, as cohorts of Cain, use denial of the evil in our collective past to avoid coming to grips with the unfinished business between Cain and Abel. We wish to avoid the difficult problem of coming to grips with the violence in our nature—that nature which is responsible for us being descendants of Cain rather than Abel. It was Cain that went on to bear children, not Abel. We choose, or are predestined, to continue to be more like Cain, even as we see that our new weapons will no longer work in the old way—kill the enemy and leave us as survivors to grab the spoils of victory. Even though the rules of war have changed forever, notwithstanding bans against the use of nuclear weapons and chemical or biological warfare, we refuse to seriously look at what has changed, and continue to assume that we can kill and reap the fruits of our killing.

Another psychological mechanism which perpetuates our violence is our tendency to project onto others, particularly those we fear, our own leanings toward violence. This justifies our violent actions, because we couch our response in terms of self-defense. During the height of the United Nations coalition's action against Iraq we heard talk of "praying for peace" from all sides. In the minds of most, this was transformed into a defensive war as we focused upon the aggression of the enemy and saw the war as a pure defense of freedom. Projection is the essential ingredient in an offensive action in order to overcome whatever scruples we have about injuring or killing others. Once we have determined that our enemy means to do us harm, self-defense justifies our deeds. This is not to say we are never in danger of attack, but projection lessens our desire to seek out our presumed opponent to see if we are in any danger and if we are being intentionally harmed.

A more primitive mental mechanism which we share with other creatures is our desire to keep what we have and acquire more if we can, without much regard for sharing it with others. The Western world has long pursued blatantly selfish policies at the expense of less developed nations. Many have said that while the conflict in the Persian Gulf was justified on the grounds of principle—non-aggression or justice or honor—depending upon which one best supported the particular argument being made at the time, the real issue was control of wealth. The United States and other Western countries want control of the wealth of the region, regardless of whether we already have more than our share. We instinctively fight someone who wants to take away what we possess, even if we have more than the person taking it.

The Race Between Utopia and Armageddon

A secure, lasting peace has to be based upon justice. Justice can only be arrived at by a process of searching out what is fair to all concerned. Many disagreements may arise among persons who sincerely seek justice, but when there is a commitment to conflict resolution by peaceful means, the tendency to protect one's possessions can be modified to achieve agreement in pursuing the common good. The human tendency to deny painful realities and to project evil motives upon others also can be limited to the point where the desire for peace wins out. But it still does not always happen.

After forty years of confrontation between two world powers we have seen them pull back from the brink. During these years of confrontation both sides developed the ultimate weapons which could essentially wipe out civilization, if not human life itself. The penetration of denial and projection played an important role in defusing the confrontation. But it was by no means complete. We may have taken a few steps toward the Utopia in which we can reason out our conflicts and extend love when reason does not reach far enough. But we have also discovered the knowledge with which we can stage Armageddon. Sooner or later we will have another conflict in which both parties have this knowledge and capability. Unless we have the will to resolve the conflict without war, we shall descend down the path we have been down many times before, only this time there will be no victor, perhaps not even a human survivor. Which will arrive first—Utopia or Armageddon?

President Bush of the United States had an unusual opportunity in 1990 to make a historic decision which might have had long-lasting consequences. Had he chosen a path that would have avoided war, the world would have backed him. He chose instead to sway public opinion in the direction of war, invoking all the time-honored devices which have been used in the past to persuade people to make war instead of peace. He said we must stop an evil man from gaining more power. Does history support this argument? The debate on this issue must now take into account the fact that if we use war as the response, we are bringing on the day of Armageddon, in addition to whatever problems we may think we are solving.

George Dyck is a psychiatrist at Prairie View, Inc., in Newton, Kansas. He received his M.D. from the University of Manitoba. During 1990, he spent three months in Jerusalem with Mennonite Central Committee.

5
Living in the Global Community

Roelf Kuitse

Christ had a deep concern for all the people he encountered, even for those who rejected him. He did not exclude his enemies from this love and from his compassionate concern.

Time and again we hear people say that we live in a global village. The world has become smaller. Events in other parts of the world have a direct impact on our way of life. Hindus, Buddhists, and Muslims are not distant neighbors anymore, living on other continents. They live among us, they are close neighbors.

Television brings the whole world into our homes. We are witnesses to wars fought in Vietnam and in the Middle East. We can see, from a distance, with our own eyes, how students in China rebel against their rulers, how empty the shelves are in Russian shops and how Muslims in Iran and Jordan express their anger against the United States.

Living together in a global village can influence us in different ways. It can broaden our horizon and help us to look at ourselves through the eyes of others. Living together can teach us tolerance and contribute to an inclusive way of thinking.

There is, however, another, more negative, possibility: the others with whom we live in our global village can be seen as a threat to our security because of their different way of thinking and acting. Feelings of insecurity can lead to exclusivism and intolerance. Closer contact with others does not always lead to better understanding.

The Middle East

In the last two decades we have had several collisions with our neighbors in the Middle East: the oil crisis in the 1970s and later the crisis with Iran over the taking of hostages. And most recently, the war with Iraq.

The Middle East is an important part of the global village. Three continents meet each other in the Middle East: Africa, Asia, and Europe. Strategically, the Middle East has played a central role in history. This is one reason why powers in the East (Soviet Union) as well as West (Britain and France) have always shown a lively interest in the Middle East.

The interest in the Middle East increased after oil was found in this region. The economies of many countries started to depend on the Middle East. Oil was regarded by many Arab Muslims as a gift of God to the Arabs, a gift that would give them again a significant role to play in history. Oil, however, turned out to be a dubious gift. This gift led to an increased, non-altruistic, interest of the outside world in the Middle East, but it also created a growing gap between the (very) rich and the poor.

The outside influence became clear after World War I. After the war, the allied forces (Britain and France) divided the region into different spheres of influence. Arbitrarily they drew boundaries, and in this way they divided the Arab nation. This was seen as an act of betrayal by Arabs. Western promises made during the war—to support the creation of one independent Arab nation— were not kept. We live in one global village with neighbors who harbor feelings of distrust against the West because of broken promises.

The United States and the Middle East

After World War II, Britain and France were displaced by the United States as the dominant power. The United States, in alliance with Iran, sought stability in the region. The Shah's Iran was provided with modern and expensive weaponry. Some of these weapons were used against the Shah's opponents in Iran.

Later, the secular dictatorship of the shah was replaced by the clerical dictatorship of the Ayatollah Khomeini. The difficulties and tensions in the Middle East and in the Islamic world were regarded by Khomeini and his followers as results of the disintegrating influence of Western culture. In the global village, we live with Muslim neighbors who see our culture as a destructive force which should be resisted by going back to the roots—the fundamental tenets—of the Islamic religion.

Iran could not be an ally of the United States after the rage of the Iranian people was directed against the United States by the taking of hostages. So the West found a new ally in Saddam Hussein's Iraq. Saddam Hussein was the protagonist of the restoration of one independent Arab nation. His attack on the new enemy, Iran, was not strongly condemned, but silently welcomed.

Yesterday's ally became today's enemy. Saddam Hussein became the enemy. Iraq's invasion of Kuwait led to the Persian Gulf War. New allies were found in Saudi Arabia and in Syria, the terrorist enemy of the past. All the allies chosen by the United States to establish stability in the Middle East have poor human rights records.

We live in one global village with neighbors whose human rights have been violated by our allies. These neighbors ask what we mean when we speak about international law and human rights.

Three Religions

The Middle East is not only strategically and economically important, it is also the birthplace of three world religions: Judaism, Christianity, and Islam. The majority of people in the Middle East are Muslims. There are Jews in Israel and small Christian minorities in almost all the countries of the Middle East.

Not all Muslims are Arabs. The majority of Muslims live in countries like Indonesia, India, Pakistan, Bangladesh, and the Soviet Union. Twenty percent of the Russian population belongs to the worldwide Islamic community. Non-Arab Muslims in the Middle East include the Iranians, Turks, and Kurds.

In spite of the fact that Arabs are a minority in the worldwide Islamic community, Arabia and the Arabic language play a significant role in that community. What happens in and around Arabia has worldwide repercussions. Islam started in Arabia. Arabs played the main role in Islamic culture during the religion's first centuries. (Later, Arabs were overshadowed by Iranians and Turks. In our time there is a resurgence of Arab nationalism.)

Five times a day Muslims perform their ritual prayers with

their faces turned in the direction of Mecca, the sacred city in Arabia. Every Muslim dreams of the day when she or he can make the pilgrimage to this city where the prophet Muhammad started his preaching. In Mecca is the sacred temple—the Kaba—which is the center of the Islamic world.

In the global village where we live together with Muslims, we should be very careful not to identify Islam with what certain leaders of countries in the Middle East are doing—even if these leaders pretend to speak and to act on behalf of the Islamic community. In times of tension, political leaders tend to use religion for their own purpose—and to justify their actions. That happens in our part of the village as well as in the Arab and Muslim part of the village.

Not all Arabs are Muslims. For many centuries Christian churches have existed in the Middle East in regions dominated by Islam. These ancient churches, which include a small minority of the population, are in a precarious situation. They are often distrusted by the Islamic community because of the tendency in the Arab community to identify Christianity with the Western world. They are also misunderstood by many Christians in the Western world as dying, ritualistic churches. Many sweeping negative statements about these churches have been made in the past without taking into consideration the special situation in which these churches have to live.

Living in a global village can make us aware of the social, political, and religious contexts in which other Christians have to live. The knowledge of, and contact with, these Christians can help us to come to a fuller understanding of the gospel. One of the challenging things in our time is that the church of Christ has become a worldwide community. Christianity cannot be identified anymore with the Western corner of the world, although there is still a tendency among many Muslims to think about Christianity in that way. In the future, Christians in non-Western parts of the world will play a significant role in the encounter with Islam.

Muslims and Christians

Believing that Christianity is *only* a Western religion is only one of the misconceptions that has to be overcome in the encounter of Muslims and Christians, if all are to live together in one global village. Muslims and Christians have a long history of misunderstanding and prejudice. Anti-Islamic feelings are part of Western tradition.

These feelings find expression in derogatory remarks about Muhammad, Islam, and the Muslims. Muhammad has been described as an imposter, as an instrument in the hands of Satan. Islam has been characterized as a religion of holy wars and polygamy, a religion running on oil. And for many Westerners, it is almost impossible to speak about Muslims without adding the adjective "fanatic." These and other negative remarks have resurfaced during the international tensions around the Middle East in the last two decades. Muslim—and Arab—bashing have become favorite games for some people. This can easily lead to dehumanization and demonization of Arabs and Muslims, which can be the first step to violent actions.

What is the background of these tendencies? Why is it that relations between Jews, Christians, and Muslims have not been better? Why does the Christian tradition have such a poor record in regard to relations with believers of the Islamic community?

Feelings of superiority on the one side and feelings of fear on the other side play a role. An attitude of superiority in regard to other cultures and religions has been part of our Western tradition for a long time. The beautiful tenets of the Christian religion were compared with the poor practices of Muslims as a way to prove the superiority of Christianity. Caricatures were made of Islam, and these caricatures were then attacked. In the beginning of this century, Islam was described as a religion in decline, a religion which would not survive the collision with Western civilization. The prophets of doom for Islam at the beginning of this century were wrong. The encounter with Western civilization has led to a resurgence of Islam. And it has become clear that Christianity is also sometimes at odds with modern civilization.

Fear has also played a role in Western attitudes toward Islam. It was a shock for people in Europe to see the fast expansion of Islam, first in Western Europe (Spain) and later in Eastern Europe (by 1683, the Muslim Turks had reached Austria). Europe did not recover from this shock for a long time. The strangeness of Islam as a religious-political community also had an impact. And Islam was seen as a dangerous competitor: it is the only post-Christian world religion. Islam claims to bring the uncorrupted message of God to the world, a message which had gotten corrupted in the hands of Christians. Islam claims to correct misunderstandings of Christians in regard to God's nature and God's will. In Islam, Christians face a religion which makes definite statements about Jesus, which differ from what Christians believe about Jesus. He is seen as one of the many human prophets preceding Muhammad, who was the last and final prophet sent into the world with the uncorrupted divine message, written down in the Qur'an, the sacred scripture of the Muslims.

The crusades were an attempt to deal with this competition in the name of God. The crusades were a violent attempt to destroy the house of Islam. Before crusaders left for the Middle East, they participated in pogroms against Jews in Europe. Persecution of Jews was an introduction to the actions against Muslims.

The crusades continued, according to Islamic views, in the colonial time. Large parts of the Islamic world were subject to the rule of European powers. That was a traumatic experience for many Muslims. Foreigners—non-Muslims—ruling in the house of Islam! What had become of God's promise that the Islamic community, as the best of all communities, would always be a victorious community? Why did history not confirm that promise anymore? Colonial rule was and is regarded as the second attempt of the Western Christian world to do harm to the Islamic community.

The third attempt, in Muslim eyes, was the creation of the state of Israel. To Muslims, Israel was the weapon of a new invasion by the West into the world of the Middle East. Arabs were paying the price for what Europeans had done to the Jews.

A Tunisian writer once wrote about "the tattooed memories" Muslims have as a result of their encounter with the West. In the global village we live together with people whose memories are tattooed by negative experiences they have had in their contacts with the West.

The Future

Living together in the global village is challenging. The global village requires cooperation in order to survive. The population explosion, the growing poverty of large parts of the world population, the ecological crisis, the increase of violence and human rights violations are issues the whole village has to deal with.

There is much distrust based on bad experiences in the past and in the present between Muslims and Christians. This distrust cannot be talked away, it can only be lived away in a common effort to respond to the challenging issues of our time.

Cooperation is only possible when we overcome exclusive

ways of thinking and acting. To think and act exclusively in the global village is dangerous. It easily leads to a division of the world into "good guys and bad guys," the "good empire and the evil empire." It is a breeding place for pride and triumphalism, for condescension in regard to others who don't think, feel, and act as we do.

Living together in a global village should lead to an inclusive way of thinking. Cooperation is only possible when we think inclusively. We need to think in ways which include the other as much as possible. We need to try to look at things through the eyes of the other so we can begin to understand where the other is. An inclusive way of thinking requires much patience and perseverance, much listening and empathy. It does not mean we have to accept everything the other does or says. If there is criticism, it should be based on understanding and not on preconceived ideas.

Inclusive thinking does not mean that one's own deepest convictions should be kept hidden. As Christians we should always be willing and ready to give positive witnesses of the hope which lives in our hearts, a hope based on the work of Jesus Christ. In Christ we see embodied this way of thinking and acting. Christ had a deep concern for all the people he encountered, even for those who rejected him. He did not exclude his enemies from this love and from his compassionate concern.

From Christ we can learn the sensitivity we need to understand others' pain and struggle, their "tattooed memories" and their feelings of betrayal. Christ can help us overcome our pride and exclusivism, our triumphalism and arrogance. In Christ we receive the courage and power to work for reconciliation, even in situations where it seems to be hopeless. Christ invites us to become partners in God's covenant against fate and the dehumanization of life. This covenant brings new life, as people are reconciled to God and to each other.

Roelf Kuitse is professor of missions at Associated Mennonite Biblical Seminaries, Elkhart, Indiana. He did his graduate studies in theology and Islamics at the University of Amsterdam and has experience teaching and in the ministry in Indonesia, Ghana, the Netherlands, and India. He has a special interest and experience in working with people of the Islamic faith.

6

Limited War in a Century of Total War

James C. Juhnke

When the bombing of Baghdad began, public opinion polls soon showed overwhelming backing for the war. People supported a war which offered military victory without apparent direct cost to the citizens.

The Persian Gulf War: A Total War?

On January 16, 1991, President George Bush announced to the American people that the nation was going to war against Iraq. He used the language of total war. The United States and its allies, the president said, would defeat the Iraqi dictator, Saddam Hussein, the new Hitler, who had "systematically raped, pillaged and plundered" the tiny nation of Kuwait. President Bush's demands were unconditional, that is, not subject to bargaining. He would accept no linkage of the problem of Kuwait to the problem of Palestine. He would not yield until he had achieved a total victory. Beyond the bright prospect of victory was nothing less than "a new world order."

Within six weeks, President Bush apparently had achieved a total military victory. First, allied bombing destroyed Iraq's infrastructure—roads, communications, and weapons facilities. Then, with casualties that were "miraculously" low, allied forces invaded and overran a demoralized Iraqi army. Jubilant news analysts proclaimed that America's superior technology, strategy, and determination had finally overcome the "Vietnam syndrome." President Bush's popular approval rating approached 90 percent. Seldom in U.S. history had opponents of war been so marginalized.

In a broader historical perspective, we do well to question whether the language of total war was appropriate to the war against Iraq. The United States sought the benefits of a total war, but without paying the costs of military conscription and taxation associated with past wars. After the fighting stopped, the meaning of the alleged total victory for the social and political future of the Middle East remained clouded. Religious pacifists, such as the Mennonites, had to readjust their witness to reflect the limited demands upon ordinary citizens in this total war context.

Century of Total War

The twentieth century has been called the century of total war. The great wars of the century, especially the World Wars of 1914-1918 and 1938-1945, demanded the absolute and unconditional defeat of the enemy. Nations in the twentieth century used all means at their disposal to achieve victory, and the means became more sophisticated and deadly with each conflict.

Total war also engaged the complete mobilization of material and spiritual resources of combating nations. Governments used their power for mass conscription of young men, as well as the power of taxation to pay for war. They controlled the mass media and manipulated national symbols to whip up popular support. Propagandists pictured the enemy as the incarnation of evil. The civilian populations joined the military crusades by increasing production and reducing consumption of food, and by volunteering for thousands of patriotic tasks that helped to win the war.

The U.S. course of total war, reaching from the Civil War to World Wars I and II through the nuclear arms race, finally reached a point of total absurdity. The stockpiles of thermonuclear weapons in the United States and the Soviet Union, and the capacity to deliver those weapons, brought the world to the brink of catastrophe. Whether it would happen by design or by accident, the next total war would destroy modern civilization. And the destruction would be caused by weapons put into place to preserve freedom.

The Origins of Total War

In the broad sweep of history, total war is a relatively recent development. A powerful tradition of war strategy stemming from the eighteenth century assumed that wars should be fought by small professional armies. Instead of seeking massive destruction, military leaders sought to achieve limited goals by occupying territory and outmaneuvering the enemy. By eighteenth-century standards, the greatest victories were those achieved with minimal killing and destruction. In the Battle of Yorktown, which ended the American War for Independence, the British commander Cornwallis surrendered to General George Washington after having been surrounded and cut off from his sources of supply. The actual casualties on both sides of that momentous battle were relatively slight.

Before the Civil War, the United States' preeminent military strategist was General Winfield Scott, who much preferred limited military combat in the eighteenth-century style. Scott's most famous campaign was the movement from Veracruz to Mexico City in the Mexican War. He attempted to avoid mass battles where possible, and enforced strict regard for the rights of enemy civilians. The war against Mexico may have begun with a questionable invasion across the Rio Grande. But the march to Mexico City involved some humane restraints typical of the earlier era of limited war.

The U.S. Civil War (1861-1865) was a transition from premodern limited war to modern total war. At the outset, nearly everyone had expected the war to be over soon, within a matter of months. But advances in military technology, especially the rifled musket, gave special advantages to defending armies. Neither side could achieve decisive victory. Each bloody battle failed to bring a conclusion. Finally the military leaders adopted a new strategy. They set aside the limits of war and adopted a strategy of annihilation.

The victorious Union general, Ulysses S. Grant, decided that the war could not be won in a single climactic battle, but by destroying the Confederate army through sustained and brutal pounding. General William T. Sherman contributed by making war on the economic means of the Confederacy to support its armies. Sherman's famous "march to the sea" assaulted the countryside as well as the will of the Southern people to continue the fight. He justified his suspension of the conventional rules and limits of war by proclaiming that "War is hell." General Grant's initials came to be identified with a doctrine of Unconditional Surrender.

Generals Grant and Sherman, exponents of the new total war strategy of annihilation, became national heroes. The belief that wars must be fought to total victory and that the enemy must yield unconditionally became firmly ingrained in American war thinking. It guided the war goals of the United States in World War I and World War II. The doctrine informed President Bush in his war against Iraq.

Total War and Democracy

The era of total war became closely identified with the ideal of democracy, especially in World War I. President Woodrow Wilson went to unprecedented lengths to involve the people in the crusade to make the world safe for democracy. He began the military draft as part of what he called "a mobilization of all the productive and active forces of the nation and their development to the highest point of cooperation and efficiency." Wilson raised money for the war through a series of popular liberty loan drives designed "to capitalize the profound impulse called patriotism." The people responded with democratic enthusiasm, volunteering to serve on local draft boards, local liberty loan committees, and local defense councils that made this the most popular of U.S. wars.

World War I demonstrated that a democratic nation engaged in total warfare is not a reliable supporter of the ideals of human freedom and minority rights. An anti-German hysteria gripped the country. Local patriot mobs went on rampages against German-speaking citizens. The national Congress passed a Sedition Act which restricted freedom of speech and press. George Kennan, diplomat and historian, compared U.S. democracy in wartime to a huge prehistoric monster with a brain the size of a pin. The beast is slow to anger, but once aroused, it "not only destroys his adversary but largely wrecks his native habitat."

Conscientious Objectors and Total War

The era of total war placed special demands upon religious groups who refused to participate in war. When nations must mobilize their entire populations for military crusades, conscientious objectors to killing must confront not only questions of combatant and noncombatant military service but of all the other quasi-military demands. Should they refuse scrap metal drives? war bond drives? planting of "victory gardens"? Issues of war and peace became so important in the twentieth century that the peace position became the definitive characteristic of pacifist groups. Mennonites were once known and labeled for their position on baptism—the Anabaptists. In the era of total war they became known as one of the "historic peace churches."

During World War I the United States was unable to develop a satisfactory system for dealing with conscientious objectors. More than 500 C.O.s were court-martialed and imprisoned. During World War II the government and the historic peace churches agreed to create the Civilian Public Service system under which C.O.s performed alternative work "in the national interest."

The experience of isolation in a nation at total war was painful. But it had a positive effect upon Mennonite identity. Because of their position on the military draft, Mennonites became more sure of their role as a distinctive people. In response to wartime challenges, they developed strong programs of service and benevolence (especially the Mennonite Central Committee) which provided a moral equivalent for war. The nation's claims upon the service and money of all citizens, together with openings for alternative service and relief work, made it possible for religious pacifists to find a generally accepted and productive place in conditions of total war.

Limited War Once Again

The nuclear arms race has made the conduct of total war obsolete. Nations have prepared for an unlimited holocaust which they dare not fight. Our wars must be limited. In Korea, Vietnam, Iraq, as well as a number of military interventions, the United States has fought military conflicts of smaller scale than the world wars which dominated the century. The United States is a superpower which has unlimited military capacity, but which has limited ability to impose political settlements.

In the context of a century of total war, one striking difference between the war against Iraq and United States' participation in World Wars I and II is that the Iraq war involved only minimal demands from the U.S. public. The great tests of popular support in total democratic warfare in 1917-18 and 1941-45 were the willingness of the people to pay for the war (through voluntary contributions or taxation) and to fight in the war (through voluntary enlistments or mass conscription).

President Bush's January 16, 1991, war address to the nation was notable for its omitting of the theme of national sacrifice. Earlier wartime presidents, Woodrow Wilson, Franklin Roosevelt, and even Lyndon Johnson, understood that genuine support for war was measured most meaningfully by the willingness of citizens to offer their money and their lives. But President Bush asked for the people's acquiescence, rather than for their sacrificial commitment. He had on hand a great stockpile of weapons built up in the 1980s under President Ronald Reagan. Total military commitment was possible without present sacrifice.

Before Bush began the battle, the people and the Congress had expressed strong reservations about war. But democracies have a remarkable ability to shift public attitudes—as the sudden war fever in 1917 had shown. When the bombing of Baghdad began, public opinion polls soon showed overwhelming backing for the war. People supported a war which offered military victory without apparent direct cost to the citizens, other than those who had voluntarily enlisted in the armed forces and reserves.

President Bush's demand for Iraq's total and unconditional surrender, however, did have some marks of total war mentality. In late February 1991, the president rejected opportunities to negotiate an orderly Iraqi withdrawal from Kuwait and instead chose to engage in a massive ground assault to destroy the Iraqi army. It remained to be seen whether Bush's accomplishment of total military victory in Iraq would be any more successful in achieving the political stability he sought, than was Woodrow Wilson's total military victory in guaranteeing a world safe for democracy. The country turned against Wilson in 1919. Would Bush's war remain popular as its hidden domestic costs and ambiguous overseas outcomes became manifest?

Weathering the Storm

The Persian Gulf War offered a new challenge to religious pacifists. In earlier times, conscientious objectors had found a niche in North American democracy geared to total war. The issue of military conscription was familiar territory. Mennonites geared up for the war with effective draft counseling programs. We can deal with a war which makes demands upon us.

But a massive technological war which lasts only a few weeks and which makes no direct claims upon citizens for service and money presents a new challenge. Conscientious objectors have been neutralized, not because war has become more just or more benign, but because the conditions of total war have been altered. The challenge now is to find a place as faithful Christians in a nation which plays out a domestically popular role as world police power without making overt sacrificial demands upon all citizens.

James C. Juhnke is professor of history at Bethel College, North Newton, Kansas. He has served in church-related assignments in West Germany, Botswana, and China, and also on the boards of Africa Inter-Mennonite Mission and the General Conference Commission on Overseas Mission. Juhnke's recent book, Vision, Doctrine, War: Mennonite Identity and Organization, 1890-1930, *is volume three in the Mennonite Experience in America series.*

7

The Economics of War

James M. Harder

*Popular consensus on the economic bene-
fits of a war economy has given politicians scant reason—let alone the
ability—to question the sky-high levels
of defense spending.*

A widely held view among citizens of the United States and
Canada is that war, however nasty in its other consequences, is
good for the economies of participant countries—unless, of
course, the war is being fought on a country's own soil. War
means plenty of jobs in aircraft, tank, and munitions factories at
home. War means a greatly expanded government payroll in the
military sector. War means that soldiers will need everything
from uniforms to freeze-dried food to medical supplies pur-
chased from tens of thousands of civilian suppliers and businesses in every part of the country.

Thus, the moral case against war aside, it is often difficult to
convince people that war might be an economic evil as well. The
economic "silver lining" view of war achieved its place in popular
culture during the 1940s, when the tremendous industrial labor
demands of World War II pulled the U.S. and Canadian economies out of the depths of the Great Depression and appeared to
usher in the prosperity of the 1950s. The wars in Korea and
Vietnam simply reinforced the home-front perception that wars

created lots of jobs and lots of profits for lots of people. This popular consensus on the economic benefits of a war economy has given politicians scant reason—let alone the ability—to question the sky-high levels of defense spending.

Nowhere is the support for ever-increasing U.S. military budgets stronger than among the 35,000 so-called prime contractors who compete for huge slices of the Pentagon's $300 billion annual budget. These civilian industries and businesses supply the 2.1 million servicemen and women of the United States and develop and produce their weapons of mass destruction. At the same time, the careers and promotions of thousands of military officers and defense department employees depend upon the success of the same prime contractors they supposedly supervise on behalf of the public's interest. The result is a clear moral hazard: a system which should contain checks and balances becomes blended into a powerful relationship of mutual interests.

Ironically, the first strong voice in recognition of this danger came from one of the United States' greatest war heroes. In his famous 1961 presidential farewell address, Dwight D. Eisenhower warned the country of the potential for a "disastrous rise of misplaced power" among the "military-industrial complex." Throughout the next three decades—during Democratic and Republican administrations alike—Eisenhower's fears have been justified. If anything, he underestimated the tendency for the military-industrial complex to be undergirded by the political process itself. The pork barrel of Pentagon spending has been crafted deliberately to make sure that each state and all congressional districts share in the spoils of military bases and equipment procurement contracts.

Public awareness and concern regarding the human and monetary costs of defense is highest during times of actual military conflict. During the 1991 Persian Gulf War, a fascinated television audience got its first glimpse of a new generation of deadly "smart" computer-guided weapons in action. Communicated by the same pictures was the tremendous cost of these wonders of technology—for example, $1.35 million for *each* of the hundreds of Tomahawk cruise missiles fired at Iraqi targets during the first few days of the war alone.

A Nation Constantly at War

In reality, however, the bulk of the cost of the Persian Gulf War will not be felt by taxpayers in 1991 or in any other single year. This is because, from an economic perspective, the United States is always at war. Prior to World War II, nations geared up for each war, then closed the munitions assembly lines and sent most of the troops home following the end of the war. Weapons of modern warfare, however, require years to research, develop, and produce. Furthermore, their sophistication dictates that large corps of professional soldiers must engage in year-round training to master the weapon systems' effective use. During the 1980s, a decade of no major wars involving the United States, fully 14.4 percent of all U.S. industrial employment was militarily related (compared to 3.9 percent in Canada), in support of a standing professional army in excess of two million soldiers. These realities underscore the fact that, in the words of disarmament economist Seymour Melman, the United States boasts a "permanent war economy."

A permanent war economy implies the ability to fight a large-scale regional war lasting many months without the need for a draft or for serious readjustment of the economy. The majority of weapons can be taken from a massive weapons inventory, which is replenished as necessary on a long-term basis. The sophisticated nature of modern weaponry—and the lead time needed to build it—may mean that no high-tech war of the future could last longer than it takes to exhaust weapon supplies on hand at the outset of the conflict. Still, the United States is well prepared. As a top executive of General Dynamics Corporation, the second largest U.S. defense contractor ($6.9 billion in 1989) observed: even if all the American tanks and planes in the Gulf War were destroyed, it would amount to only half of the weaponry already slated to be mothballed by 1995.

This tremendous stockpile of weapons did not come cheaply to the U.S. economy. Even after adjustment for inflation, military spending was 56 percent per year higher in 1989 than it had been only a decade earlier, prior to the beginning of the Reagan military buildup. In this sense, the United States has been making a down payment on the Persian Gulf War for many years (though once again, largely on credit). The effect of these bloated Pentagon peacetime budgets means that as far as the manufacturing sector goes, the exact timing of the shooting war is irrelevant; the permanent war economy can easily accommodate the regional wars of today while doing business as usual.

Viewed differently, it might seem that a permanent war economy provides the jobs, profits, and prosperity of war in even doses on a year-in and year-out basis, whether or not open hostilities are actually occurring. This perspective on a permanent war economy needs to be challenged, for it is flawed.

Sapping Life from the Economy

From an economic standpoint, a strong case can be built that the massive sums spent on military operations over a long period of time have in reality sapped, rather than strengthened, the overall health of the U.S. economy. This trend will continue, unless Pentagon budgets are dramatically slashed. Military spending is far from good for the economy. An odd alliance of sorts has formed, as many, concerned with maintaining long-term economic competitiveness, are now joining committed pacifists in calling for a substantial reduction in military spending—though certainly for different reasons.

Dollars spent on war (or on preparation for war) harm the economy in several ways. While it is true that sometimes military spending heats up the economy and thus makes inflation worse—as occurred during the Vietnam War—the main economic objections to large outlays for the Pentagon lie elsewhere.

In its broadest sense, the military's massive claim on economic resources and human talents has contributed to the relative economic decline of those countries, such as the United States and Great Britain, which commit the largest proportion of their national economic output to military purposes.

The uneven burden among nations of military spending is a major factor behind the ongoing realignment of nations in the economic world order, according to British historian Paul Kennedy in his noted book, *The Rise and Fall of the Great Powers*. In recent years, much has been made of the growing economic strength of Germany and Japan in comparison to the poor international performance of the U.S. and British economies. Throughout the 1980s, the United States and Britain each devoted from 5 to 6 percent of their respective total national output of goods and services to military purposes, compared to only 3 percent by Germany and barely 1 percent by Japan. Are these numbers pure coincidence, or are we really defending ourselves to death, economically speaking? The ways in which high military spending can result in long-term economic disadvantages for a nation are complex, but worth studying.

The most frequently heard (though probably not the most important) economic argument against spending $300 billion each year to maintain a permanent war economy focuses on the negative consequences which result in the nonmilitary private sectors of the economy. There are several ways in which huge military outlays can sap the vitality of the civilian sector of the economy. If defense spending is not paid for with current taxes but is simply added to the national debt (as 57 percent of it was during World War II, and a significant portion was during the 1980s military buildup), the government must compete against private businesses to borrow money. This increased demand for borrowed money drives up interest rates for everyone else, which reduces the amount of new productive investments which businesses can make and drives up the cost of purchasing a home, among other things. In the long run, the growth rate of the economy and standard of living slows, thanks to military spending.

Some economists have also tried to show that the Pentagon's monopoly on the services of some 30 percent of the nation's top scientists and engineers has allowed less-militarized countries such a Japan to dominate in nonmilitary technologies (for example, camcorders and compact disc players). The military's claim on innovative skill helps to explain the inability of U.S. industry to compete in world markets, it is argued. Some attempt to justify the massive drain of resources into military research and development by citing the potential for civilian spin-offs from the research—although much military research is so narrowly focused as to make civilian use highly unlikely.

While for statistical purposes the production of military hardware itself counts as an addition to the wealth of the United States, it contributes absolutely nothing to the central purpose of the economy. "Smart" bombs add neither to the present quality of living (as many consumer goods do), nor to the future standard of living (by increasing the nation's productive capacity.)

One can also examine the negative effect which military spending has on employment. A major policy objective of any nation must be to provide job opportunities for all of its citizens who wish to work. In the United States, the military-industrial complex employs 6.5 million civilian and military personnel in more than 135,000 factories, laboratories, and bases—more than 5 percent of all jobs. Worldwide an estimated 55 million people are engaged in defense-related employment. Still, studies completed in 1990 by the International Labor Organization of the United Nations found that, in general, even more jobs could be created simply by shifting government resources out of the military and into other sectors of the economy. A U.S. Bureau of Labor statistics study from 1976 supports this finding. It found that $1 billion of government spending could create 75,000 jobs in defense industries—or it could fund 100,000 jobs in construction, 138,000 jobs in the health-care field, or 187,000 jobs in education.

Shrinking Dollars for Public Spending

So far, we have focused our economic lens on the damages which military spending can inflict on the private sector of the economy. Yet, in a very real sense, high levels of military spending have depleted the public sector of the economy even more profoundly. This is perhaps the strongest argument against allocating such a large share of society's scarce resources to the military.

Since the 1950s, the government itself has laid claim to a remarkably stable 20 percent share of the economy's total goods and services (combining total federal, state, and local government purchases). During the 1980s, a 6.1 percent share was taken for military purposes, state and local government units used 11.7 percent of the economy's output, and an astonishingly low *2.2 percent* of the nation's output represented all resources available at the federal level for nonmilitary purchases (excluding items such as Social Security and unemployment compensation, which are really not government spending at all, but rather a transfer of wealth from one private citizen to another).

This small 2.2 percent slice of the nation's output—down from a 4 percent share in the 1960s—was stretched to cover many needs and programs: promotion of commerce, operation of national forests and parks, acquisition and disposal of agricultural commodities, construction of flood control projects, operation of the federal air control system, medical research on AIDS, law enforcement, new investment in the postal service and Amtrak, space exploration, and the list goes on. Nearly all these programs, however small, were cut by the Carter and Reagan administrations. After adjustment for the effects of inflation, military purchases still rose by 64 percent during this period, while federal nonmilitary purchases actually declined by 4 percent. State and local governments did not take up the slack; their purchases actually dropped as a percentage of the nation's annual output.

A Crumbling Economic Framework

This declining rate of nonmilitary public spending during the past fifteen to twenty years—induced by the political decision to divert more and more federal dollars into the military and enforced by legislated limits on total government spending—has left the nation's basic economic and social framework, or infrastructure in a dilapidated condition. The consequences of this decline in public funding include underfunded education and medical research, and deteriorated streets, highways, bridges, mass transit systems, railways, public housing sites, waste disposal systems, jails and prisons. At the same time that public investment in the future has been declining, the economy has greatly expanded, dumping a tremendous burden of environmental damage, transportation congestion, and urban abandonment on an overwhelmed and underfunded public sector.

This trend increasingly threatens the social well-being of the people that the military is supposedly there to protect. It has serious implications for growth and future prosperity. It has been estimated that every dollar invested in public infrastructure adds four dollars to the total national output within only five years because it helps the economy to operate more efficiently. From 1973 to 1985, the United States devoted less than 0.3 percent of annual output to maintaining and improving its infrastructure, whereas Japan spent 5 percent. As one result, the Japanese economy is twice as energy efficient as that of the United States—which means that Japanese industry can produce at lower cost and win the war of economic competition.

The United States was drawn into the Persian Gulf War primarily to protect its self-described vital interest of access to cheap oil. Contrary to popular belief, Japan had no need for that war to be fought, in spite of its total dependence on imported oil. This is because Japan's superior investment in public infrastructure and energy efficiency guarantees its ability to compete with other economies, no matter what the worldwide price of oil. How many more natural resource wars might the United States feel it needs to fight in the future for much the same reason? The self-imposed U.S. burden of military might has indeed sapped its ability to compete in the new global economic order.

While the benefits to national security are vigorously championed, they are in no sense explained in terms of the damage to the economy inflicted by deep budget cuts in nonmilitary public programs. Even the annual military budget figures published by official Washington do not reflect the true costs to society of the military burden. Official figures place the military budget at only a quarter of total federal spending for fiscal year 1991. In reality, the proportion of federal expenditures (excluding Social Security and similar trust funds) committed to military-related causes is much higher. The Friends Committee on National Legislation includes military aid to foreign governments, NASA's direct military spending, veterans and military pension benefits, and interest payments on the military portion of the national debt in calculating that fully 52 percent of all federal spending has a military price tag attached to it. Approximately 16 percent of the federal budget goes merely to pay the interest on that portion (58.3 percent) of the nation's $2.2 trillion debt which is a result of *past* military spending. Without this obligation, the current annual budget deficit would be nearly eliminated.

High Costs, Low Benefits

Military spending both hinders economic vitality and causes a particular kind of economy to develop. It imposes high economic costs on all, but yields economic benefits to only scattered special interests. Other spending priorities, other technological emphases and other types of job patterns are not only possible, but would yield a healthier and more broadly based economy in the long run than we have at present under the permanent war economy.

To shift away from the status quo will not be easy. Economic changes always yield both individual and regional winners and losers—although a sharp reduction in military spending would ultimately create far more winners than losers. It is true that significant reduction of defense spending would devastate employment possibilities for a few highly specialized scientists. The economies of some towns—which have enjoyed large military payrolls for years—would be ruined when military bases or factories close down. The twelve states in the "gun belt" along both coasts and across the south which together boast 64 percent of all civilian defense-related jobs would feel the pinch far more than other states (similar to the experience of some states during the 1980s farm crisis). Yet in all cases, the total gains to society due to a healthier economy would exceed the total losses to individuals.

Political realities suggest that the military-industrial complex and its permanent war economy will not yield easily to change. The end of the Cold War and perennial domestic budget crises will likely combine to eliminate as many as one million defense-related jobs by 1995. Activists in the "economic conversion" movement are searching for ways to speed the process by finding peaceful uses for existing defense plants and employees. Any transition will be made even more politically difficult by the fact that its costs will be felt immediately, while most benefits would be of a longer term nature. Yet the evidence strongly suggests that the nation should demand change. The strong moral arguments against war aside, a purely economic case can be made that it is in the interest of the United States to devote a far smaller share of its scarce public resources to maintaining its military might.

James M. Harder is assistant professor of economics at Bethel College in North Newton, Kansas. He received his Ph.D. in development economics from the University of Notre Dame. Before coming to Bethel, he served in East Africa for four years under Mennonite Central Committee and Mennonite Economic Development Associates.

8

Mass Media and War

Stuart W. Showalter

Despite the public's perception of North American mass media as critical watchdogs over government, research indicates the opposite: the media more often resemble friendly lapdogs who attend loyally to the government's beck and call.

Television's evening news began routinely enough on January 16, 1991, but viewers, along with the network anchors, soon sensed that a major story was breaking. Field reports transmitted from Dhahran, Saudi Arabia, featured correspondents speaking over the deafening noise of departing fighter-bombers. Later that evening, reporters for Cable News Network (CNN) dramatically described bombs bursting in air over Baghdad, Iraq. Eventually, everybody realized that the United States and its allies had launched a massive air assault in the Middle East. On the spot, television news programs were transformed into special reports which ran uninterrupted for hours.

In the days and weeks ahead, the Persian Gulf War preoccupied journalists, and people everywhere eagerly sought the latest news. Television networks could broadcast for the first time specific incidents of conflict as they unfolded, a feat made possible by the orbiting of communications satellites above the earth. TV viewers in North America watched missiles colliding in midair while Saudi civilians witnessed these same scenes from their rooftops in Riyadh.

Although modern technologies have changed both military tactics and journalistic practices, questions about mass media's role in responding to modern warfare remain fundamental:

• How do the news media generate public opinion supportive of national leaders' goals in wartime?
• How does public opinion influence the nature of mass media coverage of war?
• How do presidents, military commanders, and press secretaries control the flow of information?
• How much freedom should reporters have in reporting what they know from the war front?
• What responsibility do reporters have to present dissenters' points of view during wartime?
• To what or to whom do professional journalists owe their ultimate allegiance? The truth? Their audience? Their employer? Their country or cause?

These questions lie behind the mass media's role in shaping the North American political climate during wartime. Despite the public's perception of North American mass media as critical watchdogs over government, research indicates the opposite: the media more often resemble friendly lapdogs who attend loyally to the government's beck and call.

Three Models of Mass Media Effects

When radio developed in the first half of the twentieth century, the public considered this new medium a powerful instrument of persuasion. Indeed, radio commercials in the 1920s helped stimulate a strong postwar consumer economy. When that economy collapsed into the Great Depression, President Franklin Roosevelt gave his famous "Fireside Chats" on radio to aid in the recovery. In Germany, meanwhile, Adolf Hitler also relied on radio to rally support for his misguided political and military goals before and during World War II.

Radio, which gave the public a new electronic link to the outside world, both delighted and frightened its millions of listeners in the 1930s and 1940s. Fear arose especially from reports of how Hitler was mobilizing Germany for war, and both scholars and the public consequently perceived radio as a powerful instrument of propaganda. In the 1930s an institute for propaganda analysis identified seven propaganda devices and educated a receptive public to their manipulative potential.

These experiences with radio led scholars to think of the mass media as all-powerful, a model which seemed attractive and had vigorous supporters into the 1950s. However, when researchers attempted to document the flow of strong influence from mass media to the public, they found the connection a weak one. Much more important in forming values and influencing decision making, they discovered, were the ways individuals related personally to others, primarily family members and co-workers. This line of research, which achieved its strongest influence in the late 1950s and early 1960s, viewed the media as largely neutral. In this limited effects model, media consumers constituted an "obstinate audience" who were capable of selectively accepting or rejecting persuasive appeals. Persuasive communications were given the power only to reinforce existing values and behaviors whose origins supposedly lay quite outside the media mainstream.

A third model of mass media influence, labeled agenda-setting, emerged in the late 1960s as a response to both the powerful effects and limited effects models. Mass media are not all-powerful, the agenda setters acknowledged. On the other hand, they argued, why would businesses and politicians spend billions of dollars annually to advertise products or leadership potential if the media simply reinforced existing beliefs? The agenda-setting scholars, using data from mass media coverage of election campaigns, concluded that over a period of time the media can shape matters of public concern.

So viewpoints spread widely and repeatedly in the mass media, like water dripping from stalactites in a cave, do influence society. In his book *Inventing Reality*, political scientist Michael Parenti describes the process this way: "The media have a great deal of power in controlling *opinion visibility*. They create a media image of public opinion that often plays a more crucial role in setting the issue agenda than does actual public opinion." This agenda-setting model of mass media influence has been accepted widely by both those who study mass media and those working in media.

The Mass Media and Marketplace Forces

Agenda setting must be considered in the context of its economic structure, including the profit-oriented structure favored by mass media in the West. Critical consumers of news realize that profit frequently determines editorial and program choices. The popular media generate their profits chiefly from advertising (commercial radio and television, newspapers, and magazines) or direct sales (movies and books). The size and type of circulation directly affects the rates newspapers and magazines can charge for advertising space. Similarly, Nielsen and Arbitron ratings measure the size and type of audiences for broadcasters. Because advertising income has a pronounced relationship with profitability, media managers pay special attention to barometers of public opinion and adjust their content continually in an effort to attract the biggest audience in a given market.

In the 1980s the thirst for profits resulted in large-scale economic consolidation among the mass media, not unlike mergers in other industries. For example, in 1989 Time, Inc., and Warner Communications merged to form the United States' largest media company, one that generates more than $6 billion annually in revenues. Among the Time-Warner companies are magazines, book publishing houses, film studios and movies, and far-flung cable television systems. Even more troubling for some critics are the interlocking ownership ties between major corporations which have both media and non-media holdings. For example, the NBC radio and television network is a subsidiary of electronics giant RCA, which in turn is owned by General Electric, which manufactures engines for some military jet aircraft. Such connections have the obvious potential for calling into question a news network's credibility.

Group-owned newspapers also threaten journalistic independence and integrity. In the United States, corporate chains such as Gannett and Knight-Ridder, not local publishers, control three-fourths of all daily newspaper circulation. Such consolidation has turned the mass media into near-facsimiles of each other. A dull, middle-America sameness characterizes the mass media more than the democratic ideal of a vigorous marketplace of competing ideas.

An alternate economic structure for mass media is government ownership and control. Indeed, today many countries own and operate mass media channels, especially radio and television systems. However, government ownership has barely gained a foothold in North America, aside from the respected Canadian Broadcasting Corporation. Government ownership also has its limitations, including chronic fund shortages and little appreciation for the needs and aspirations of audiences. Most negatively, some governments exercise strict control over their mass media by assigning censors to serve as gatekeepers of message content.

Television as an Agenda-Setter in the Gulf War

Among the North American mass media, television clearly dominates. Nearly 99 percent of the households have at least one TV set. In the United States (figures for Canada are similar), a television set in the average household is switched on for more than seven hours daily. Adults watch 2.5 hours of TV daily, while children average 4.5 hours.

During the Persian Gulf War, TV viewers spent lots of time in front of their sets. Soon after the air war began, Cable News Network, owing to its around-the-clock coverage and ongoing presence in Baghdad, saw its ratings zoom upward nearly 300 percent. (CNN also gained an enhanced journalistic reputation, spurred a flood of orders for household hookups of cable TV, and increased its prime-time advertising rates 500 percent within a month.) Another indicator that the public followed the war avidly was the fact that ABC's "Night Line" with Ted Koppel surpassed in ratings the perennial leader, "The Tonight Show" with Johnny Carson. Finally, a study among children in Israel, where incoming Iraqi missiles caused the schools to close for several weeks, found that they watched up to nine hours of television daily, double the average.

What images did the TV viewers see?

For one thing, they became accustomed to the on-screen presence of the world's dominant political leaders. President George Bush quickly emerged as the West's chief advocate for using military force. Behind the scenes, he had forged a coalition of thirty-eight nations and had won the assent of the United Nations and the U.S. Congress to confront Iraq militarily. Publicly, he argued the case for a just war in a variety of forums—from informal replies to journalists' shouted questions to his State of the Union address, with the television cameras always rolling.

By building international and domestic support for his position, Bush structured the ideological agenda for war and projected an image of unity and strength that undercut his critics. One measure of the effectiveness of his communication was sharply soaring approval ratings in national public opinion polls. They rose from 57 percent in December 1990 to 77 percent in mid-

January to 85 percent in late February after the cease-fire was announced.

Taking a cue from the president were his leading military advisors, namely the secretary of defense, the chairman of the joint chiefs of staff, and the commander of the coalition forces. In their televised interviews and press conferences, they presented a unified voice on the information front. General Norman Schwarzkopf, the coalition commander, and his military colleagues became familiar figures as they parried with the press in briefings. They were especially impressive when they supplemented their prepared statements with videotape footage of "direct hits" by laser-guided bombs on Iraqi targets—footage that resembled a Nintendo game more than the terrible reality of war. *Newsweek's* media critic wryly observed that the war on TV was "strangely bloodless."

Muzzles on the Mass Media in Wartime

In the twentieth century, American journalists have operated under censorship in every major war they have covered, with much of the censorship being voluntary and self-imposed. Restricting press freedom in wartime gained a legal precedent set in World War I by the U.S. Supreme Court. Justice Oliver Wendell Holmes devised the "clear and present danger" argument and wrote, "When a nation is at war many things that might be said in time of peace are such a hindrance to its effort that their utterance will not be endured."

Media-wise public affairs specialists, such as Pete Williams from the U.S. department of defense, didn't leave censorship to chance in the Persian Gulf theater. They formulated detailed policies governing military-media interaction. These public relations professionals won approval from their political and military superiors for guidelines that kept the would-be watchdogs on a short leash. The days of reporters' roaming the war zone freely, as many had done in Vietnam, had ended. News of on-location military action was limited to stories supplied by small "pools" of reporters who represented their colleagues. So, at the war's peak, perhaps 120 reporters with military escorts served as the eyes and ears for a contingent of more than 800 colleagues.

By controlling the flow of information, the military could largely limit reporters and editors to sanitized versions of what was happening in the field. Invariably in wartime, the government's public relations practitioners inflate the amount of damage inflicted on the enemy and minimize the losses experienced by the side providing the information. Reporters, without the opportunity to verify the assessments provided by the military itself, were left to write or say primarily what they were told. True, some resorted to speculation, which lessens a medium's credibility, and a few moved out to find stories on their own. Reporters in the latter category, such as Bob Simon of CBS and Peter Arnett of CNN, risked capture by opposing forces or criticism from government officials and the public.

The military further restricted coverage by making rules about the types of photographs and information considered off-limits and unwelcome. Only after the cease-fire went into effect did the world learn that as many as 150,000 Iraqis were killed in the war. In regard to the lack of casualty reports, one columnist observed, "Americans have been watching TV so long and have grown so accustomed to commercial and political packaging and wish-fulfilling explanations of painful public issues that they simply cannot stand the truth."

Reporters routinely encountered official censorship in stories filed from Saudi Arabia, Israel, and Iraq. While the stated reason for censorship in wartime is increased security for a nation's military forces, the underlying motivation in modern warfare is just as likely to be political. The trade journal *Editor & Publisher* noted that "numerous security reviews have involved more editing than reviewing, for example, changing the word 'anxiously' to 'alertly.' " Censors also delayed stories for a day or two, greatly reducing their timeliness.

While some journalists complained about censorship, the American public strongly endorsed the way the military handled reporters in the Persian Gulf War and even encouraged more control. Results from a *Times Mirror* poll in late January revealed that 57 percent of the respondents said they thought the military should exert more control over how news media reported the conflict. By contrast, one-third of the respondents said journalists were more qualified to judge how to report on the war.

As for interpreting the war, journalists seemed quite willing to adopt much of the coalition leaders' vocabulary. The very names of missiles and planes—for example, *Patriot* and *Eagle*—had built-in positive connotations. Officers assigned bombing missions a fancy French noun, *sortie*, which the public learned to use from hearing it so often on radio and television. A vague term such as *collateral damage* did not diminish the terror and pain civilians must have felt when enemy bombs exploded nearby. *Friendly fire* was deadly fire when it struck a fellow soldier.

Once the air war began, journalists joined the public in applauding the war effort, their obligation to provide diverse viewpoints seemingly forgotten. The *Newsweek* media critic noted the lack of counter-perspectives on the war: "Only rarely [were] Iraqi refugees who fled to Jordan . . . interviewed on TV about the effects of the allied bombing, as if firsthand accounts of war [were] somehow less newsworthy than the 'I've got nothing for you on that' comments of briefers or the repetitious speculation of retired generals. Dissenters from the war, given at least a little voice before hostilities began, [were] all but absent from most network coverage."

The Lack of Dissent in the Mass Media

Pacifists of all stripes failed to make much of an impact through the mass media during the Persian Gulf War. Coalition leaders did such an effective job in enlisting support for their position that peace groups found little appreciation for their minority viewpoint. Even a rally of approximately 300,000 protesters who marched in Washington, D.C., on January 26 attracted little more than fleeting spot coverage.

Dissenters found it difficult to express their convictions in other ways. For example, little American flag patches sprouted up overnight on the uniforms of major college basketball teams. At Seton Hall University in New Jersey, one player declined to wear the flag because he said this gesture violated his Christian beliefs. Fans harassed the player and his pregnant wife to the point that he quit the team and left the country. In the Pacific Coast Conference, only the University of California basketball team initially chose not to wear patches or yellow ribbons. "Suppose it [the war] doesn't turn out well?" asked the chancellor. Soon, however, the university delegated the decision to individual players, and the entire team chose the flags. Television, of course, prominently displayed the patches.

On the radio, disc jockeys played over and over patriotic music such as "The Star-Spangled Banner" and Lee Greenwood's "God Bless the USA." Getting a lot less attention were songs such as "War Is Hell on the Homefront." One program director said, "You don't want to knock the troops or anything like that." One Big Band station was so sensitive to public opinion that management yanked an instrumental piece called "In a Persian

Market." Even the internationally minded British Broadcasting Corporation banned several songs deemed controversial, including the late John Lennon's "Give Peace a Chance."

Conclusion

Citizens in the United States have indicated repeatedly that they cherish "freedom of the press," guaranteed by the First Amendment, as one of the nation's fundamental ideals. In practice, however, mainstream mass media are highly conformist, partly in response to perceived public preferences. Such conformity, accentuated in wartime, puts great pressure on those whose convictions run counter to national policy. They must turn to less powerful "alternative media" to express their viewpoints and be unusually creative in gaining a hearing for their divergent opinions.

In a democratic society, citizens who have a vision for another way in wartime might not be heard in the mass media at all. Minority voices are especially diminished if the war, like the one in the Persian Gulf, is short and, from the perspective of political and military elites, sweet.

Stuart W. Showalter is professor of communication at Goshen College, where he also chairs the communication department. His doctoral dissertation, completed in 1975 at the University of Texas at Austin, focuses on American magazine coverage of conscientious objectors to the Vietnam War.

9

War and the Elementary Classroom

Norma Peters Duerksen

Teachers for years have had to deal with crises of many types. . . . Most crises do not challenge moral beliefs, however, like war does.

War, like a bouncy ball, has a tendency to bounce out of control, ricocheting off one object and glancing off the next. Each hit along its path leaves the victim hurting. This uncaring monster also bounces into school buildings, down the hall, crazily careening into each classroom to create its bruises and pain on each student trying to study. As if it finds energy from each encounter, it sails from room to room, from office to lounge, where its drumming of victims leaves chaos. Some cheer in support of the acrobatic stunts this ball can do and some mourn the bruises, not only within their walls, but around the world. The ball bounces crazily out the door to destinations unknown.

So it seems that war enters classrooms across the nations. News of the starting of war leaves one non-functional. One cannot study or work due to disbelief, worry, and grief. Students of all ages are affected when their parents or loved ones are called on to serve in the armed forces. There is a separation that can only be filled with tender loving care.

A child comes to school scared and confused. He wants his family back together like normal. Yet, he believes his parents must be right, in being there to fight, "so blow the enemy off the map" and get it over with, he says.

A third-grader comes to a special education class and leans over the table ignoring the carefully displayed teaching items laid out for instruction. She begins to share what is on her mind. She tells of family on the front lines in the war. She asks about many of her fears. Will they bomb my house? Are we going to be killed? The materials set out on the table for that day's lesson are never touched during that class period. What can one learn when one needs a listening ear and a safe place to share?

The topic of war has not come up in any conversations in a first grade classroom. One, however, needs only to observe the students' play at recess to realize that the war is very much on their minds. Stocking caps are transformed into gas masks as they fit over their faces. After much play shooting and reactive death collapsing on the ground by boys and girls alike, it seems to become real in the minds of these young students. One thoughtful child approaches the teacher on recess duty and voices her concern. "I don't think we should play war anymore. It is much more serious than this," she says.

Sometimes religious views creep into the discussions of students. One confident fourth-grader joyfully reports, "You know we're going to win—it's written in the Bible." What do teachers say when students come with not only different political views but also different religious views?

As the school day begins, a group of students gather around a boy who holds a sheet of paper in his hand. There is laughter; loud comments are made that attract the attention of the teacher at her desk. When she approaches the group of students at the back of the room, the students disband, leaving the lone child holding the paper. As the teacher gets closer she notices that the paper shows an enlarged picture of Saddam Hussein overlaid with a bull's-eye target. All eyes are on the teacher as to what her response will be.

Dealing with questions and comments of students is difficult when one's personal views are different than the majority opinion in society. School mandated policies make it even harder in the classroom.

When the Teacher Is in the Minority

One Monday morning a kindergarten teacher comes to school to find that the decision has been made to play the national anthem, followed by the reciting of the country's pledge of allegiance, over the intercom. Every classroom in the whole building will join in the singing and reciting of these nationalistic pieces at the same time. In an area near an air force base, many of these kindergarten students are not able to sleep at night. They worry about the war reports on TV, knowing a parent is in the war zone. They must sing the words "bombs bursting in air," which occurs in the national anthem, every morning.

Friday is to be Peace Day at school. Everyone is to wear the national colors of red, white, and blue. The directive to the classroom teachers is for each class to produce something yellow, a color showing support for the troops at war.

An all-school assembly is scheduled. The presenter will be a military person describing the bombers and other intriguing machinery being used in the war. Do pacifist teachers take their classes to this assembly? What would happen if they didn't? Will there be an all-school assembly about the enemy's side of the issue? Is there an assembly concerning peacemaking?

Another all-school assembly calls everyone to the front lawn of the school. Classes present some nationalistic reading, poem, song, or skit. These are followed by the ceremonious tying of large yellow ribbons around each tree in the front yard of the school in honor of military personnel fighting overseas. Everyone joins in the singing of "God Bless America." As classes dismiss to return to their classrooms inside, they are to pass a crisp yellow ribbon tied to a tree and pause to place their hand on this symbol of support.

Teachers for years have had to deal with crises of many types—providing counseling, a sympathetic ear, and tender loving care. Most crises do not challenge the moral beliefs, however, like war does. To pacifists, war seems like an avoidable crisis, which makes it hard to support and talk about without bias in the classroom.

Facts are easier to deal with than emotions. As teachers scramble for facts of the countries involved, they only find old, yellowed documents of outdated maps and information. Again we realize that we lack knowledge of the rest of the world. Becoming aware is the first task, and yet truth is the first thing to go in every war. Where does one go for information? It seems that a mixture of sources will be the only way to get more than one side to the issues. The church resources give perspectives of people in Christian service working closely with the victims of war. The government news shows up in many periodicals and news releases. This balance of information is important to help open the teachers' and students' eyes to more than one side of the issue.

One thing is clear—the war affects every classroom, not just the social studies or history classes. English classes write letters to the soldiers out on the battlefield. The students make the connection with actual people. These letter exchanges show the human side of the conflict. Daily casualty lists on the news are met with rapt attention by these pen pals.

Math classes try to deal with how many soldiers, how many tanks, or how much money is being spent on the war. Graphs with cut-out symbols representing every 100 units cover classroom walls. Such huge numbers must raise either pride or questions in children's minds.

Dealing with students is only half of the struggle for a teacher who is pacifist. Down the hall, in the teachers' lounge, discussions with co-workers can also be painful.

When the Teachers' Lounge Feels Like Enemy Territory

Flags are being sold in the lounge. One fervent war-supporting colleague asks the pacifist whether he has bought his flag yet. How does one respond on the spur of the moment?

Some children in a pacifist teacher's classroom decide to wear peace slogans instead of flags and yellow ribbons. Teachers of another persuasion voice their concern as to how such disloyalty can be allowed.

On a rare occasion a pacifist teacher finds a colleague with differing views with whom to dialogue. The point is not to state one's beliefs and run, but to talk openly and honestly without the relationship falling apart. Two such teachers find the chance for such a dialogue over lunch in the teacher's lounge. Another teacher passes through the room to pick up a sack lunch from the refrigerator. She leaves and reports the war dialogue to the principal, who reprimands them for offending people by their conversation.

Upon obviously conveying pacifist views, a teacher is greeted with such verbal abuse that she does not go to the lounge anymore. Such tension causes headaches.

Teachers seek to allow free expression of views, including their own. Knowing that no setting is value-neutral, one seeks to promote discussion and respect for other people's opinions from kindergarten on through the years.

Even if the temptation is strong to avoid all controversial talk of war, actions and reactions speak louder than words. Not allowing a target to be made of *any* human being, including Saddam Hussein, teaches respect. Students may question the teacher's loyalty to the national cause; teachers may then express love for one's country but not for its actions in a given situation. If not feeling threatened, a teacher can discuss being not only citizens of one particular nation but being citizens of the world.

Timing is important. The feelings of the class must be gauged to know when tensions are too high and need to be diffused. Further discussion should be postponed to a less emotionally packed moment.

Teaching About Peace

War tends to magnify the need for a positive sense of self-worth, for concern for others, for skills in conflict resolution, and for global awareness. These needs can be addressed every day, every year—war or no war.

Some schools have adopted a peace curriculum for their public school classrooms. This curriculum helps students examine an active life-enhancing meaning of peace. Research by Educators for Social Responsibility (ESR) shows that many young people have a clear conception of war, while their conceptions of peace are vague. "Often students see peace as dull, passive, or as merely the absence of war." School peace curricula do not strive to define peace but allow students to grapple with the issue in order to clarify their own understanding of peace.

Through experiential learning students discover that peace can be exciting and creative. Peace involves action, accomplishment, power, joy, and unity with other humans. Peace encourages the use of cooperative behavior, learning to work together better.

Such a curriculum, as recommended by ESR, also studies the obstacles to peace: fear, aggression, stereotyping, prejudice, ideology, and propaganda. Fear and anger are not necessarily bad. A lack of legitimate expressions of these emotions is what causes conflicts within oneself and among others.

In order for learning to occur, we often put things into categories. However, categorizing to the point of holding negative conceptions of groups of people is usually due to misinformation or lack of experience with them. Prejudice occurs when stereotyping of groups of people turns negative. One group no longer sees the other as complex, desirable, friendly, or unique.

This view of the world leads to an ideology of exclusivism. One sees only one's own views as correct. It distorts how one sees and hears people of other views. To get others to join one's view, one resorts to the use of propaganda. In this way, one tries to control the attitudes and actions of others.

Educators for Social Responsibility states that these obstacles to peace are real, but all are created by humans. Therefore, the teacher and students are faced with the possibility of removing these obstacles from the paths of peace.

Having been helped to define peace and to explore the obstacles to peace, students and teachers are ready to learn conflict resolution. There are many people whose lives can be studied that exemplify skills of conflict resolution. These "peace heroes" can give hope to a student cynical about possibilities of anything changing. Cynical despair, prevalent in many youth today, can be addressed by peace curricula that give them skills for change and allow their youthful idealism to create a vision for the future.

One can only hope that a teacher's efforts to engage students actively in the topic of war and peace will help the students develop a sense of control—control over a crazily bouncing ball that with wisdom and skill can be caught and returned to its box.

Norma Peters Duerksen, Goessel, Kansas, serves as secretary for children's education for the General Conference Mennonite Church. Her teaching experience includes nine years in public schools and two years in a voluntary service assignment. She has been involved in preaching, teaching, serving as a deacon, and in clown ministry.

10
War, Peace, and the Workplace

Doug Penner

When emotions are running high, we may feel that we are forced to choose between our personal convictions and our relationships with co-workers.

A couple of weeks after the 1991 coalition aerial attacks on Iraq and Kuwait had begun, the pastor of my home church delivered a sermon based on Psalm 137. There, the psalmist speaks the familiar words of pain and anger of a people in exile, "By the rivers of Babylon, there we sat down and we wept, when we remembered Zion."

In these words our pastor identified some of the feelings of grief and separation that many feel today when we oppose a war that is supported by a large majority of those around us. The passions of patriotism, duty, and conscience begin to separate us from people we've lived and worked closely with for years, and we begin to feel like strangers in familiar places surrounded by familiar faces. This can be particularly true in our work lives, where, perhaps unlike our church and family lives, pacifism is more likely a minority position. In settings like these, we begin to search for ways in which we can be what we wish our national leaders would be in their relationships with other nations: makers of peace and justice.

Two kinds of issues may be of special concern for people facing workplace conflicts over issues of war and peace: 1) dealing with the interpersonal issues that arise when we are committed to a position that differs sharply from that of our co-workers, and 2) managing the personal stresses and turmoil that accompany these conflicts.

Dealing with Issues That Divide

When emotions are running high, we may feel that we are forced to choose between our personal convictions and our relationships with co-workers. If we see ourselves as committed to our positions, our employers, and our work, we may not feel we have the option of strongly advocating a position that co-workers regard as virtual treason. At the same time, we may feel weak or dishonest if we don't speak out on issues that are at the core of our Christian beliefs. The dilemma is real, and the pain it creates can be powerful. During the first weeks of the air war against Iraq, teachers in Newton, Kansas, told of avoiding the coffee room because of the accusatory atmosphere they knew they would find there, of dreading to go to school, and of leaving for home each day with intense headaches and other physical symptoms.

In the midst of these kinds of interpersonal strains, it may be helpful to be aware of a few general principles related to conflict and peacemaking. These principles are based on two assumptions: 1) that our commitments to peace and justice are as relevant to personal relationships as they are to relationships between nations, and 2) that positive things can happen when people are able to engage in honest, direct discussion of issues they disagree about and still maintain a relationship.

1. Peacemaking at the interpersonal level involves a variety of skills and actions. Timing is an important issue in choosing how to act towards co-workers with whom we disagree. There are times when efforts to talk about issues seem to deteriorate almost automatically into hostile exchanges. During these times, people seem to talk past each other, neither hearing nor appreciating others' points of view. After such an encounter, we may feel that we've been honest about our convictions, but we may also recognize that we've contributed to polarization of a tense situation, but contributed little to understanding. Or, because we find such encounters intimidating and unpleasant, we keep quiet, feeling afterward like hypocritical cowards.

When we face these kinds of circumstances, it may be helpful to think about peacemaking and conflict management as involving skills such as making judgments about the best times and ways to speak out, and the best times and ways not to speak out.

A popular image of conflict management that incorporates this idea suggests that there are two broad kinds of activities involved in working through disagreements. One is a set of skills and attitudes that includes communicating our own position, advocating that position, and pressing for its understanding and acceptance. These kinds of skills are often called "assertive" behaviors.

The second broad set of actions involves things like listening to the other party's position, accepting parts of it that make sense to us, expressing our agreement, and communicating our openness and respect. These are referred to as "supportive" behaviors.

Being entirely assertive in a conflict situation would often mean being true to personal convictions, but might mean giving up any kind of relationship with the party we disagree with. Being entirely supportive would usually mean preserving the relationship but sacrificing commitment to something we believe in.

In the midst of the kind of personal and interpersonal turmoil presented by being a minority pacifist, it may be helpful to recognize that there is no single, simple way of being a peacemaker. Honest commitment to peacemaking that takes into account both international and interpersonal relations allows for the possibility of a wide range of actions. Often this will mean blending assertive and supportive behaviors, but sometimes it will mean relying heavily on one or the other of the styles. A strong visible expression of opposition to war, of alternative ways of resolving national differences, of global and other national perspectives on the issues will be constructive at times. At other times, listening, hearing perspectives that contrast with ours, and expressing recognition and empathy for other points of view will be timely. Being effective peacemakers in the world means developing these skills and the wisdom to use them in the most productive ways.

2. While the intensity of feelings involved in these conflicts usually makes them feel very personal, what happens when conflict grows is, in some respects, a predictable social process to which all participants are victims. It has been demonstrated again and again, from the national to the small group level, that when groups come into conflict, they tend to move systematically towards behaviors and attitudes that intensify conflict and

animosity.

- Simpler and clearer images develop that portray "us" as correct and moral, and "them" as wrong and immoral. Information that doesn't fit these images is likely to be ignored or distorted.
- Issues increasingly are viewed as simple, and black and white.
- Communication between parties is reduced, making it easier to maintain simple, either/or images.
- Neutrality becomes less and less acceptable.

When we are faced with intense conflicts about war, it may be useful to recognize ways in which these kinds of things might be happening to us. Doing this may make it more possible to react to "them" as reasonable, honest, well-intentioned people. It may allow us to react in ways that set the stage for meaningful discussion of issues, including assertion of a pacifist point of view and pacifist alternatives to war. The alternative—viewing oneself as surrounded by irrational, immoral, defensive people—is likely to be neither personally nor interpersonally productive.

Managing Stress and Turmoil

The second broad area involved in facing issues of war in the workplace has to do with personal responses. Pacifists who face the visible reality of war and experience its impact on relationships and routines in their lives soon start to recognize their own unique indicators—emotional, physical, and interpersonal—of being stressed. Without being aware of it, we can gradually shift into a prolonged state of emotional and physical tension that will eventually exact some kind of toll.

There is no complete way to "cope one's way out" of the felt strain of this kind of situation. The pain of being in the minority, and of confronting the awful face of war, is unavoidable. Recognizing that contemporary pacifists suffer little when compared with previous generations or with pacifists in other countries helps put current experiences in perspective, but doesn't necessarily change the day-to-day experience. The grief, the pain—even the shame—are real.

In the midst of these feelings, attention to spiritual needs strikes me as particularly important. For some, giving more time to prayer, reflection, and meditation is an effective step. Others find connection with the artist's response in music, visual art, and drama. The traditional Negro spirituals, born out of generations of suffering and separation, seem to communicate with special power.

There are, however, some general ways of approaching the stresses of workplace conflict about war that offer the possibility of minimizing distress and physical and emotional harm. Several have to do with how we interpret events and our experiences of them.

Research on the nature and consequences of stress has concluded that one aspect of the experience of stress is particularly important. A feeling of powerlessness in the face of events seems to intensify the physical and psychological impact of stress. The less we feel we have the ability to influence difficult events, the more likely we are to be and to feel stressed.

This issue takes on a special significance when military events unfold as rapidly and mechanically as they did in the war in Iraq. People described a feeling of utter helplessness as the war proceeded, and as neighbors, co-workers, and school children took their own personal steps to express their support for the government's military response. It is probably realistic to feel generally powerless in the face of circumstances like these. It is only healthy to see that there are some things upon which we are likely to have little impact.

But some of our actions do have the possibility of having an impact, even if very small. It is psychologically and practically important to identify these things and focus our efforts on carrying them out, rather than allowing ourselves to feel overwhelmed by the scope of uncontrollable events going on around us. Writing letters and calling government officials, participating in public witness, giving support to organizations pressing for alternative solutions, giving financial support for programs aimed at giving aid to victims of war, and a host of other actions take on special significance at times like these.

Turning Threats into Challenges

A second related way in which our interpretations can influence how we experience the workplace strains of war is through our tendency to regard these difficulties as either threatening or challenging. The difference between these two perceptions is an important one, because they can result in different degrees of stress. An event viewed as threatening seems to trigger a set of other additional perceptions, physical and emotional reactions, and, most importantly, coping responses that are potentially more harmful. The same event viewed as a challenge is more likely to lead to a set of more positive reactions. Most important, coping responses are more likely to be oriented towards solving problems rather than avoiding them.

The differences between these interpretations become more meaningful when we recognize that in many circumstances, our experiences are ambiguous enough that we can choose what kind of interpretation we will make. Workplace conflicts offer us the chance to look at difficulties as opportunities for personal growth—opportunities for strengthening belief systems, improving abilities to deal with differences, widening our understanding of complex issues.

Finally, we need to recognize the role played by supportive relationships in helping us through difficult times. There is a body of research which suggests that the availability of close supportive relationships helps people to deal with physical and psychological stressors in their lives. Simply put, feeling isolated tends to open us to the damage stress can cause. When war issues strain our relationships with some at work, it becomes much more important that we be able to turn to other individuals and to groups to help us explore and understand what we are experiencing, and to simply communicate their concern for our well-being. At the same time, it becomes more important for each person to recognize the support role that they are capable of playing in the lives of those around them. Sunday school classes, shepherd groups, family members, and close friends can be powerful sources of strength in turbulent times.

These kinds of general principles and strategies for managing the difficulties that war brings to the workplace offer, I hope, the possibility of responding with personal conviction and integrity, with a commitment to community, and in ways that work for peace and justice in distant places, in our communities, and in our personal relationships.

Doug Penner is a social psychologist who serves as Executive Director for the Associated Colleges of Central Kansas. He earned a Ph.D. from the University of Kansas. A former professor of psychology at Bethel College, North Newton, Kansas, Penner taught in China under the China Educational Exchange program. He has also done organizational consulting with Prairie View Growth Associates, Newton, Kansas.

11
Peacemakers Confronted

Robert Hull

With the social clocks turned back fifty years, many "patriots" again see North America's wars as moral crusades. . . . How then do we Christian peacemakers communicate our convictions? How do we confront the intimidation to silence?

"The times they are a-changin'," was the energizing Bob Dylan line in the 1960s. For many of us, the "times" of North American culture certainly seem to have changed.

Seemingly forgotten are the efforts at sensitivity toward racial minorities. People of other nations, and even North Americans who happen to be poor, are the objects of disdain. We hear words such as *loser* or *nerd* or *faggot*. We catch phrases such as *to Jew him down* or *dumb as a Polack (U.S.)* or *dumb as a Newfie (Canada)*.

I believe the "Reagan Revolution" was the source of much of this latter-day callousness. The growing economic differences between the truly needy and the truly greedy accelerated. They were blessed and justified by "the bulliest pulpit in the land," the presidency itself. The Great Communicator could somehow never find words fit to bind the nation together in dignity and unity of purpose.

Regarding both national legislation and many social issues, the "Reagan Revolution" in the United States and the Mulroney landslide election in Canada turned the North American social clocks back fifty years. It is as if the former erased the liberalism of Franklin Roosevelt's New Deal. It is as if the New Democratic Party had never emerged as a liberal third voice in Canada. National leaders no longer lift up the making of social progress in areas of sensitivity, equality, and fairness as major national goals.

Then August 2, 1990, burst upon us. The army of Iraq invaded and occupied Kuwait. For five months, the United States and Canada prepared for war. They joined an international coalition of some thirty other nations. On January 16, 1991, they launched an air war against Iraq. On February 23, a ground campaign followed. In less than a week, the war was over. The military strength of Iraq crumbled, and the coalition "freed" Kuwait to return to its monarchical government.

At home in the United States, flags flew everywhere. Oversize bows and ribbons festooned every village. "Supporting our troops until they come home" was the unspoken message. One could purchase one's very own "America kicks butt" lapel button in the local supermarket. Strident patriots disrupted peace vigils and shouted down Christian hymns, chanting "U-S-A, U-S-A, U-S-A!" Less strident disruption occurred in Canada, to Canadians' credit.

Thoughtful but contrary perspectives seemingly disappeared from North American television, radio, and newspapers. Talk show hosts were ecstatic—their special brand of "my country right or wrong" jingoism had seldom been so popular. Letters to the editor carrying a similar message appeared in many papers: "Once the war has begun, any dissent is traitorous. Those people should be locked up for the duration!" The Republican National Committee, no less, mailed out 500,000 pre-printed and pre-addressed "Letters to the Editor" (*Newsweek* Magazine, March 4, 1991). Republican supporters were instructed to complain that the media had devoted *too much* coverage to the small number of antiwar protesters!

For many peacemakers, this wartime North America seems like a prison under "lock-down" rules. The newly popular habit of equating dissent with treason reminds us of World War I. We miss the relative tolerance of diversity we felt during the Vietnam War. Can you imagine the response if we conducted our worship services in Arabic in 1991? (Many of our grandparents faced similar hostility when they worshiped in German in 1917-18.)

With the social clocks turned back fifty years, many "patriots"

again see North America's wars as moral crusades. They aggressively confront today's peacemakers with the realities of an economic draft. Social progress? Why, the military offers the best
equal opportunity for minorities to obtain upward mobility! we
hear people say.

How then do we Christian peacemakers communicate our convictions? What is the goal? How do we confront the intimidation
to silence, while not contributing to provocation?

The Goal

Our goal, above all else, must be dialogue. For it is only through
dialogue that we can hope to persuade others with integrity. Our
integrity must identify us as peacemakers. Such integrity often
means, in specific terms, letting the results fall as they may.

Ronald C. Arnett, a Church of the Brethren member, described
the goal of dialogue for peacemakers. His book, *Dwell in Peace:
Applying Nonviolence to Everyday Relationships*, concludes with
two chapters, "Confronting in Dialogue" and "The Dialogue of
Peace." Arnett explores first the philosophy of the Jewish writer,
Martin Buber, and his famous "I and Thou" perspective. Then
Arnett favorably compares Buber's speech-based philosophy of
dialogue with Mohandas Gandhi's action-based philosophy of
conflict resolution (*satyagraha*).

Our agenda for peacemaking emerges from Buber's perspective on dialogue and Gandhi's perspective on conflict resolution.

Each party in a confrontation must voice his or her view assert-
ively, while openly attempting to understand the others' perspectives. Each holds to his or her view until persuaded to
modify it. Thus, each party serves the others by providing a key
perspective they may not have considered. By being open to the
others' perspectives, each party suggests that he or she does not
have *all* the truth.

Dialogue differs from debate; there is skillful balance between
the assertiveness, which characterizes debate, and openness.
Dialogue is not a matter of win one point and lose another, until
someone judges that the preponderance of points clearly favors
one side. Then it is winner-take-all and the debate concludes.

In the genuine dialogue we seek, each party assumes that no
one brings the complete solution to the confrontation. This openness characterizes genuine dialogue. The parties fully expect the
solution to emerge "between" them. They expect it to be not
totally like the initial perspectives of any of them.

Mohandas Gandhi practiced a similar set of assumptions and expectations. He frequently dealt with larger-scale confrontations of social conflict. In *Conquest of Violence*, Joan V. Bondurant says:

> The objective of satyagraha is to win victory over the conflict situation—to discover further truths and to persuade the opponent. Holding to the truth means holding to what the satyagrahi believes to be the truth until he or she is dissuaded from that position or part of it. Perhaps the most characteristic quality of satyagraha is the flexibility in ends which an emphasis on means implies. His [or her] dogma—if such a thing can be alleged—lies in adherence to a means, to a technique, which has specific moral elements at its base. But what action in these terms may mean—what it may lead to as a social, or political, or individual end—is highly unpredictable (p. viii).

Almost all of us find seeking victory *over the conflict situation* an innovative perspective. Our societies have traditionally prepared us to win victory *over the opponent*. According to Arnett, Martin Buber and Mohandas Gandhi offer a breakthrough to the peacemaker. She or he must conceive the resolution to a conflict as a property of the relationships involved. The resolution is never the property of one party to the conflict. It "belongs" to the relationships established in the dialogue. Each party shares in, but does not solely own, the final, joint resolution.

As our peacemaking attempts to follow Buber and Gandhi in their dialogue and conflict resolution philosophies, it is unlikely it will produce similar results in any two conflict situations. Indeed, Buber and Gandhi had their own disagreements. Both involved themselves in their historical situations, as Buber responded to the Nazi oppression of the Jewish people and Gandhi responded to the British oppression of the Indian people. In their famous correspondence, later made public, Buber said Gandhi did not understand Nazi totalitarianism. Buber claimed its methods differed from British imperialism. Gandhi nevertheless contended that *satyagraha* could have been effective against the Nazis. Buber and Gandhi did not produce arguments that won over the other. They sought to deepen their understanding and further develop their own perspective from the exchange.

One Significant Effort

Christian Peacemaker Teams (CPT) is a major peacemaking initiative sponsored by the General Conference Mennonite Church, Church of the Brethren, Mennonite Church, and Brethren in Christ Church since 1986. CPT took its dialogue form of peacemaking to Baghdad in late November 1990. Among its delegation were Mennonites and Brethren with a total of more than thirty years of experience in the Middle East.

The historical situation at that time was very intense emotionally. Iraq's occupation of Kuwait was brutal. Iraqi troops publicly executed resistance fighters and engaged in widespread pillaging and raping. In addition, Iraq held almost 1,000 civilian hostages and had stationed some of them at military and industrial targets.

For its side, the position of the international coalition opposing Iraq was massively threatening. On center stage was an ongoing military buildup, which eventually reached 530,000 combatants. The United Nations Security Council was approving a series of resolutions. They approved the final resolution (authorizing the use of military force) on November 30, while the Christian Peacemaker Team was still in Baghdad. The U.N. resolutions did not embargo food and medicine, but the international coalition's blockades were having this effect. Above all, the position of the U.S. president, claiming to speak for the coalition, remained unchanged. There were to be no negotiations toward any goal other than unconditional withdrawal.

CPT sought to find some opening for dialogue. The CPT delegation's message to the Iraqi officials was candid. "Your annexation of Kuwait cannot be justified, and must end immediately. Your holding of civilian hostages likewise cannot be justified. It tends to inflame public opinion in our countries (the United States and Canada) against you." At the same time, the team listened to the Iraqi grievances against Kuwait. They heard their pleas that the embargo of food and medicines hurt the vulnerable children, the poor, and the ill the most.

The Christian Peacemaker Team promised that several of them would visit Washington and Ottawa when they returned to North America. All of them promised to speak to the media in an effort to get the food and medicine blockades lifted. They hoped to remove the intensely emotional issues of hostages, food, and medicine from the conflict agenda. Perhaps then there could be an opening for a meaningful dialogue through negotiations. As a gesture of goodwill, the Iraqi government released five hostages to follow the CPT delegation back to North America. Five days later they announced the release of all the hostages. For their part, the various international coalition governments sent several emissaries to Baghdad in the succeeding weeks. However, the international coalition did not lift the food and medicine blockade. The public rhetoric of the coalition leaders said the emissaries were not negotiators. They claimed they were merely personal conveyers of the same "unconditional withdrawal" message.

The result of the CPT delegation's journey was clearly never in their hands. The confrontation did not end as they had hoped. It was, nevertheless, just as clearly an effort worth making.

The Means: Peacemaking Skills

I believe that the people in the CPT delegation did their best. They represented some of the best of current peace church resource people. Their dialogue efforts closely approached the necessary balance between assertiveness and openness.

The peace churches have solidly begun an exploration of nonviolent peacemaking. They now sponsor such initiatives as the Christian Peacemaker Teams, the Mennonite and the Brethren Conciliation Services, the various college peace studies programs, and a historical understanding of the value of respect for relationships in conflict resolution.

As peacemakers, our next steps are to strengthen our skills of *communication*, including candor, paraphrasing, active listening, and assertiveness. We must acquire skills of *organizing* for effective consultation and for rapid response. We must develop skills of *nonviolence* to pursue our goals with consensus and plan our strategies and tactics with integrity. Finally, we must renew our skills—if we may call them that—of *faith*. We must trust in God's providence and have confidence in God's will for peace as the fruit of justice. Again and again, we must seek God's grace as our source for courage.

The 1990s are a new historical situation for peacemaking. Indications are that rampant militarism and triumphalism in North American societies will be the norm. We will need to refine many peacemaking skills in order to move through confrontation to effective dialogue. Blessed are the peacemakers who shall take up such tasks.

Robert Hull is secretary for peace and justice of the General Conference Mennonite Church. Since 1989, he has served as chairperson of the Christian Peacemaker Teams steering committee. In the summer and fall of 1990, he worked with CPT peacemaking efforts during the Mohawk crisis in Quebec.

12
Becoming Friends with the Enemy

Dorothy Friesen

George Bush and his public relations team were successful in moving people in the United States to support the Persian Gulf War, partly through their appeal to the deeply-embedded racism in our society.

"Christian communities will not allow the government to define who their enemies are." *Harry Huebner, Christian Peacemaker Team (CPT) member, speaking at a press conference in Baghdad, November 1990*

"What does it mean to put a face on the enemy? It implies— seeing life through their eyes, feeling their fear and pain, walking in their shoes, perceiving reality from their point of view, thinking, reasoning, understanding how their minds work, opening our hearts wide." *Hedy Sawadsky, Christian Peacemaker Team—Ontario*

Public support for the Persian Gulf War provided a vivid example of how easily people in North America are swayed by government rhetoric and media propaganda. Our governments were able to manufacture an enemy in short order—Iraqi president Saddam Hussein, a leader who had been an ally only a few years ago.

Thus, even though there were indications that a negotiated settlement was possible almost as soon as Iraq invaded Kuwait in the beginning of August, the U.S. government was able to rebuff peace overtures over a six-month period without appearing to be the aggressor to the majority of its citizens.

Simplistic analysis and insecurity sparked public support for bombing missions—even if it meant thousands of Iraqi civilian casualties. Yellow ribbons and flags hung everywhere, focusing concern for *our* troops only. An avalanche of rainbow ribbons to symbolize our common humanity did not appear. After the war the destruction of Kuwait was described in detail; the destruction of Baghdad and the two hundred thousand or more Iraqi dead were not mentioned.

There is clearly fertile ground among the populations of Canada and the United States for the villainization of a single leader, as well as a readiness to jump on anyone else in our society who might look like "the enemy." Bush's publicists appealed to the racism and provincialism of the people. Canadian Prime Minister Mulroney followed every U.S. move with enthusiasm, including the questioning (read "harassment") of Canadians of Arab descent.

What we experienced in January and February of 1991 laid bare the challenge for peace people in North America. We are not only dealing with the greed and the systematic defense of the rich (whether in the West or in the Arab world) or with the myopia and cultural blinders of our leadership. Even the majority of the ordinary citizens who did not benefit from the war in the Middle East accepted that war and some even vehemently supported it. According to public opinion polls, fewer women and African-Americans supported the war. However, the bombardment of media messages can effectively shape even the opinion of the disenfranchised and separate it from their daily experience.

How can we develop critical thinking so we will not be swept along by government pronouncements? How can we build confidence so that we can withstand our leaders' appeals to the authority of their position or national security? Most importantly, how can people of peace promote a wider appreciation of the sacredness of all humanity—white, black, American, Canadian, Iraqi, Kuwaiti, or Palestinian?

There are two levels of work to be done to befriend the "enemy."

Immediate Short-Term Response

In the short term, acting clearly against our government's war is a sign of friendship to the victims of that war in other countries. During the Persian Gulf crisis, for example, the Christian Peacemaker Teams, an initiative of the Mennonite, Church of the Brethren, and Brethren in Christ denominations, visited Iraq.

Leila Sharif, Jordanian Senate member, addressed the CPT members in Amman, Jordan, before they entered Iraq: "The essential thing in your role in the United States is to describe the Iraqis as people, not monsters. The issue is complex. Convey to the Iraqis that you are not their enemies." While the team was in Iraq they were told by Adnan Daud Solomon, minister without portfolio in the Iraqi Assembly and chair of the Commission for Peace and Solidarity, "Your visit is important. Hear us. We sense the language of understanding as we look into your eyes. Help us have greater understanding in the United States and other nations."

Meanwhile, in the United States and Canada, hundreds of Mennonite congregations participated in Christian Peacemaker Team activities aimed at averting the war in the gulf. Perhaps more than in any war before, Mennonite people across the country—from the nations' capitals and large cities to rural Iowa and Saskatchewan—were on the streets and in the media in their local communities making their voices heard.

Another short-term act of friendship in our local communities is to respond immediately to defend persons who are the targets of threat and harassment, simply because our government is at war with their country of origin. For example, during the Persian Gulf War, it became more important than usual to seek out North Americans of Arab descent, precisely because they were targets of both government and private citizen harassment. Since August 1990, the American Arab Anti-Discrimination Committee and other groups around the United States have documented hundreds of threats and acts of violence against Arab Americans, including death threats, physical assaults, and vandalism. Arab Americans also came under increasing harassment by the Federal Bureau of Investigation who questioned them as though they were terrorists.

We can speak out against discriminatory acts or acts of violence which occur in our community by raising the issue in our local congregations, in community forums, in discussions with our neighbors, and in letters to our local papers. Our response makes harassment unacceptable and insures that it doesn't happen again.

It is also important to seek out the victims and let them know that we do not agree with what is happening. During the Persian Gulf crisis, Arab shopkeepers in Chicago felt attacked and many tried to lay low. They could have used friendly encouragement and a sense that they were not alone. The best defense for a people is to stand up and be proud of who they are. We can invite targeted persons to tell their story, if they are willing, to our church group or Sunday school class. Then, as a group, we can decide appropriate action to take to make our support clear.

Incidents against specific persons did not happen everywhere. However, all of us, no matter where we lived, witnessed the negative dehumanizing images of Arabs projected in cartoons, on television, and on talk radio shows. At the time, it may have seemed too overwhelming to answer such a barrage. But even a modest public response to one cartoon can give courage to others who are also uncomfortable with stereotyping, but were afraid to speak up. If we are too shy to call a radio talk show, we can write a short note to the radio station or newspaper, pointing out their bias or presenting an alternative view.

Taking active steps to learn about another culture is an act of friendship. Seeking out people in our own communities who come from a country with which our government is at war helps us to learn about their culture and their view of what is happening. In larger cities, it is not difficult to find people of Arab descent. Palestinians are everywhere since they have no homeland of their own.

In smaller towns it may be more difficult, but even in rural areas there is a growing multiculturalism in Canada and in the United States. If there is no one in our town, we can inquire about international students at local colleges or universities. Invite more than one person or encourage your guest to bring a friend. It can be intimidating for a guest to walk into a roomful of strangers who are different from them and talk about their homeland.

Before we invite someone to share with our church or neighborhood group, it helps to consult a map and encyclopedia for some basic knowledge. Making the effort to get some knowledge on our own is a sign of respect to the person we have invited and will make the first few moments of meeting a little easier. U.S. citizens particularly have a notorious reputation for not knowing anything about any other country other than their own.

A little research on our part can help to break a stereotype. Sometimes there are returned missionaries or international development workers in our communities who can provide information about the current country out of favor with our government. They can act as a bridge, but it is very important to interact with the people of another culture directly. Knowing a flesh and blood person underlines our common humanity in an unforgettable way.

If the invited guests feel better just answering questions, be prepared. The art of asking questions is important to making the relationship work. The common tasks of life make good opening questions: What do people eat? How do they get their staple foods? How is the food prepared? Questions on natural environment could include: What are common kinds of flowers? birds? plants? trees? landscape? How do people dress? What are the common means of travel? What does a typical day look like for a rural or city person? What is celebrated in the society and how? How are passages of life—birth, marriage, death—marked? After the stage has been set, the deeper questions of religious belief and customs and political views can be elicited.

If the guest would like to give a talk, you could suggest some things you think your group would like to know. Maybe she or he could bring an item of food, clothing, a tape of music, or some other artifact which can help convey a part of the culture and worldview. If there are children in your group, sharing games or songs can be fun and it helps to loosen up people. It is important for both children and adults to understand the contributions which our government's current "enemy" have made to civilization.

Mennonites have sometimes been called a musical people. Coming to appreciate the music of another culture is a way of extending the hand of peace. Violent and inhuman behavior toward a people is less tolerated once we have appreciated their music and eaten their food.

In Chicago, we sponsored a half-day conference on the Middle East and asked an Assyrian family we knew to make an Iraqi meal. Before they came, the father said, "We are a little bit afraid. Do you think the people at the conference will hate us?" The family outdid themselves, presenting a ten-course meal, to the delight of the conference attendees. The family was proud to show off their food. People in Chicago got a sense of the wide array of the delicious food of Iraq. Cookbooks are available if you cannot find someone from the Middle East in your town. During the Vietnam War, for example, the Indo-China Mobile Education Project used food very effectively. In addition to a speaker and photo display about the life of Vietnamese people, the project supplied written step-by-step directions to local hosts on how to make a simple Vietnamese dish. Food, nourishment, and the common breaking of bread are important ways to establish relationships. The local church is a good place to host these cross-cultural meals. The church, after all, is a sanctuary for people—a meeting place of various expressions of God's creation.

If there are no resource persons in the community, local colleges, or in a nearby city, educational resources like books, films, videos, or slide shows can be ordered from local libraries, Mennonite Central Committee, or other Mennonite offices. (A good resource on the Middle East is *Arab World Notebook*, Secondary School Level, edited by Audrey Shabbas and Ayed Al-Qazzaz, 1989; 350 pages in 3-ring-style; $39.95. Available from NAJDA Women Concerned about the Middle East, 1400 Shattuck Avenue, Suite 7, Berkeley, CA 94709; 412-549-3512. The notebook is full of information, resources, film/video/booklists and helpful suggestions for methods of using the material. Some materials are adapted from church-based books and articles.)

Long-Term Work: Undoing Racism

George Bush and his public relations team were successful in moving people in the United States to support the Persian Gulf War, partly through their appeal to the deeply-embedded racism in our society. A monocultural view of the world, in which Euro-America is the norm, is particularly dangerous since Euro-America is the society in a position to militarily wipe out others different from it.

In contrast, befriending the enemy builds on the notion that every culture reflects the image of God. We miss the completeness of God's creation if we consciously or unconsciously assume that our culture is the norm and that no other is equally precious. The journey from a monocultural view to a genuine treasuring of what another culture offers is the most important step of friendship. This means working to understand the effect of white-skin privilege in our society, and working to undo white supremacy assumptions in ourselves and our society. This hit me forcefully during a neighborhood meeting soon after the Persian Gulf War ended. (I live in a predominantly African-American neighborhood on the West Side of Chicago, where people struggle every day for jobs, for housing, for schools.) Someone handed out posters designed by a neighboring Catholic parish which said, "Arabs are not our enemies; Arabs are our friends." Peace was written in several languages around the poster. The posters elicited explosive comments around the table. One person said, "Why didn't they put out a poster which said, 'African-Americans are not our enemies; African Americans are our friends.'? We have been raped, beaten, lynched, killed, harassed, discriminated against for hundreds of years. No one put out a poster for us." If it had been a native American meeting, someone could have asked a similar question.

Arab friendship posters were an important response at a time when 100,000 Arabs were killed by our troops, but my neighbor's reaction was also on target. The same treatment of Arabs in the United States and Canada—acts of harassment, discrimination, and violence against individuals, as well as generally negative, stereotypical or non-images in the media—continues against African Americans.

During the war, there was a big jump in incidents against Arab persons and Jewish synagogues and properties, but statistically, the greatest number of discriminatory incidents are still directed towards African Americans. The war in the gulf lasted six weeks; the war against the poor and the people of color in this country continues to be waged.

Black people are often stereotypically presented as our enemies—welfare cheats, drug users, and criminals—whom we have to imprison or kill. The demented mindset which can approve killing thousands and then call the war "low casualty," is the same mind which can pull the plug on essential services in the inner city, disrupt communities and call it "urban redevelopment." Bush successfully appealed to the accumulated fear and prejudice with his Willie Horton commercials during the 1988 presidential campaign. He continued that strategy, targeting Noriega when the United States invaded in Panama and then targeting Hussein as an excuse for his Middle East adventure.

We can and must stop the cycle at home. We can follow the same steps of getting to know another people as human beings whose culture opens to us a part of the image of God to which we might not otherwise have access. Reading African American and native American history, novels, poetry; listening to music; attending cultural and church events; inviting people to our homes or church gatherings; speaking clearly against acts of racist violence; recognizing and challenging negative stereotypes; confessing our historical complicity in oppression; supporting restitution: these are all acts of friendship.

As we do the long-term work of befriending the "enemy" at home, we also gain experience so we can more resolutely resist the next international "enemy" our government presents to us.

Dorothy Friesen of Chicago, Illinois, is one of the founders and current director of Synapses, an interfaith action network which links domestic and international issues of justice. She and her husband, Gene Stoltz-fus, were Mennonite Central Committee representatives in the Philippines from 1977 to 1979.

13
Crisis Care for Young Children

Rosella Wiens Regier

For forty-two days of war in 1991, parents and care givers of very young children tried to provide the best understanding and support possible. . . . They cherished the children and dealt with their concerns. And the children taught us all as well.

"I do not like war. But if Saddam Hussein gets out, we will not have war. I do not believe in war," wrote a six-year-old. This is such inclusive wisdom in three short statements of personal feelings, war strategy, and religious convictions.

Thirteen days later, the coalition forces backed by the United Nations declared war on Iraq. From before January 16 and even after February 27, 1991, children around the world tried to make sense of world events. They struggled openly and honestly, sometimes in painful silence. They were eloquent in their expressions as they searched for answers to a pain that wouldn't go away.

"I like the dark best when the lights are on," said Dennis the Menace. For forty-two days of war in 1991, though the light was very dim, parents and care givers of very young children tried to provide the best understanding and support possible. They coped with the routine of daily life, practiced Christian peacemaking, and viewed the world through global perspectives. They cherished the children and dealt with their concerns. And the children taught us all as well.

Coping with the Routine of Daily Life

1. *Be Aware of Stress Factors*

A two-year-old was eating supper with his parents when suddenly he said, "Not good." His mother thought he didn't like something he was eating, and she said, "What's not good?" Earnestly he replied, "War's not good." She was startled since war had not been openly discussed in his presence. Then his dad remembered that several days earlier they had talked about the pictures of the Persian Gulf War on television and he told his son, "War is not good."

Several years ago, when the subject of nuclear bombing was so current, a seven-year-old girl asked her adult friend at church, "When all the world gets smashed, and everybody dies, who is going to bury me?" Her friend wisely said: "There doesn't have to be a war. That's why it's so important that those of us who believe in peace really work hard for peace. And I want to assure you. One thing I know is that no matter where you are and even if there are bad times, God will always be with you."

Another child said during the 1991 war that his stomach felt like it was full of butterflies, moths, wasps, and bees and that he was afraid they would all fly up out of his mouth and begin to sting him.

2. *Reassure Children of Care*

In any fearful time, children need to know they are safe and being cared for. They need to be able to trust the adults in their lives. In a televised message to parents during the war, Fred Rogers said that "children don't make wars so the least—and the best—we adults can do is to let our children know that we'll take good care of them no matter what."

A primary school-aged child had trouble getting to sleep at night. He had bags under his eyes. When his parents talked to him about it, he said he didn't know why. His father tells the story:

> One evening, about ten minutes after we had put our eight-year-old to bed, he came downstairs from his bedroom and said, "I just remembered why I can't sleep. I keep think-

ing about death."

"Are you afraid you're going to die?" I asked.

"No. I think about whether I'll have a long death or a short death." His voice cracked, his eyes filled with tears. He sat on his mother's lap.

"What do you mean?"

"Like if I get sick and it takes me a long time to die."

"And a short death would be if you died suddenly, like in an accident?"

"Yeah."

"Would you rather have a short death?"

"Yeah."

"Are you afraid of what'll happen to you after you die?" my wife asked.

"Not really."

"What will happen?"

"I'll go to heaven I guess."

On a hunch, I asked if the war made him think about these things. Yes, he said, it did.

"Do you talk about it at school?"

"No, not much. But some people have relatives over there."

"And you're afraid they might die?"

"Yeah."

"It's a scary thing," we agreed. "Would you like to pray about it?"

"Okay."

We sat together, touched him, and prayed. We asked the Lord to take away his fear, to help him get to sleep, to know that he is safe.

At the end of the prayer, I said, "Son, look at me. Your mom and I will do everything we can to keep you from getting hurt. Okay?"

"Uh-huh."

I walked back upstairs with him. I asked if he'd like to have a picture of Jesus beside his bed to help him remember that Jesus is always with him. He said he would. We hugged. I kissed him, and he returned the kiss.

Since that night, he has not had trouble going to sleep.

3. *Encourage Honest Expression of Feelings*

A pacifist teacher in Manitoba encouraged her second-graders to write in their journals. She responds to their writing with notes of her own. One child wrote: "I don't like war, do you? The stealth bomber looked cool. This might be World War 3. I don't like war. Do you? Sometimes war gives me bad feelings. The jets look cool. So do the tanks." And the teacher responded: "War gives me bad feelings too. The jets and tanks look cool, but they kill people and that's not cool."

Very young children may not have language skills to express their feelings verbally. We can help them deal with their feelings through dramatic play, with crayons or clay, or puppets. Adults can provide a sense of security by genuinely listening and accepting unconditionally the feelings and experiences portrayed by the children.

4. *Apply Principles of Conflict Resolution*

An experienced parent who relates to young children in her home day-care center in Central Kansas says she is convinced that children need to learn early about peacemaking. With six children in her care, there are numerous opportunities to practice conflict resolution. She follows at least four principles with the children:

  a. *Discuss.* "Let's talk about this," she says. Then each child is given an uninterrupted chance to tell what happened.

  b. *Compromise.* Generally, an agreeable compromise is reached between the children.

  c. *Negotiate.* Specific requests may be made: "I don't like it when you hit me. Please don't do it again."

  d. *Resolution.* Responses of children may be agreement, and also sometimes apology.

This care giver knew her attempts at teaching peacemaking were working when she heard a child threaten to "tell" during a conflict. The second child responded: "No, we're supposed to talk it over."

5. *Talk Together with the Children*

Pediatrician T. Berry Brazelton, nationally known author and editor, suggests adults share difficult information with children in ways that allow their questions to surface, perhaps setting up special times each day or week and saying: "Well, now it's time for us to talk about what's going on. What are your questions" (*Newsweek*, February 25, 1991, page 52). Sharing information in a family setting is important. Children know or sense what's going on and can't be protected from all knowledge, especially when they start school. Giving them handles for coping, understanding, and interpreting world events is critical. During Desert Storm, Fred Rogers, on "Mister Roger's Neighborhood," gave children handles. Talk to adults whom you love, he told children, about your fears and feelings. And children did. When some boys began throwing bombs as they played war, the adult caring for them explained as simply as she could the Persian Gulf situation. Eventually one of them advised: "They should have talked it over instead of fighting."

A family with older children spent an evening in Bible study, looking at Scriptures for assurance and comfort. Through discussion together, the children asked questions and gained insights to incorporate into their school life later on.

6. Maintain Family Rituals

A four-year-old experienced trauma at the death of her favorite aunt. On the way to the memorial service, the little girl insisted on reading books. Especially during that stressful time, she needed to follow the favorite family ritual of reading books while in the car.

A youngster who was seven always ended his prayers with the same line: "And please, dear God, help it to be a nice day tomorrow." When his parents asked him why he did it, he said, "I like the same closing every day."

The very young need and enjoy the practice of predictable routines. They insist on a certain way "we always do it" at bedtime, during story time, or at meals. These rituals validate their being. Familiar routines help them know that the world, as they know it, is predictable; that the people, as they experience them, can be depended upon. During stressful times, there is comfort in normalcy, in something solid they can count on.

7. Limit Television

A five-year-old said, "Teacher, are you going home to watch the war?"

For young children who watch horror and death and destruction on television, the line between reality and fantasy is blurred. War is not a game to be turned off and on with the flick of a switch or the press of a button. Care givers are encouraged to limit unsupervised television and to turn the set off at times. Instead, conversations or activities about the crisis or war are encouraged. If children watch difficult material—with or without adults—care must be taken to process the conflicts, and time must be given to answering questions and dealing with issues.

8. Avoid War Toys

A large toy company executive suggests that toys tend to mirror what happens in the real society. "Whatever parents are into, the kids want to be into, too," he said.

At the eighty-eighth annual American International Toy Fair in early 1991, it was possible to learn a lot about our world. Two hot topics in toyland were war and saving the planet from ecological disaster. Desert Storm produced explosions in toy departments. The F-117A Stealth Bomber sales soared 300 percent in the early weeks of the Iraqi war. International demands for a new strategy game were so great that manufacturers worked around the clock to produce it.

Peacemakers, on the other hand, have the opportunity to purchase toys that teach children to save our planet from industrial pollution. These toys might include stuffed toys with environmental messages, purchasing or making stuffed globes and maps designed to teach children about the world, or using cooperative games.

Sometimes there is terror in the toy box. John Redekop suggests seven ways Christian families can intentionally counterbalance the effects of violence through toy choices for children:

a. Don't buy any war toys.
b. Destroy—don't give away—any war toys in the house.
c. Write to makers of war toys. Express and suggest they promote more suitable alternatives.
d. Take time to teach children the Christian emphasis on peace and the value of a human life.
e. Provide alternative games and toys. (One such company is Animal Town Game Co., Box 2002, Santa Barbara, CA 93120.)
f. Monitor television; explain why certain programs should not be viewed.
g. Personally model and promote the better Christian way.

(*Gospel Herald*, May 24, 1988, page 357, reprinted from *MB Herald*)

Practicing Christian Peacemaking

9. Root Children in Faith

A five-year-old child in Nebraska talked to his Sunday school class and teacher about an uncle who participated in alternative service and a grandpa who was a conscientious objector, both in earlier war conflicts. The teacher talked to his mother and discovered that during the time the child constantly wanted to play war, the family took the opportunity to discuss family beliefs.

During the Persian Gulf crisis, a third-grade Sunday school class in Ohio studied the Old Testament character, Gideon. The teacher used the opportunity to discuss and compare the biblical material to current experience of conflict as well.

When a seven-year-old and his school classmates in Nebraska were asked to send cards and some Kool-Aid to United States troops in Saudi Arabia, the child's card included "support for the war and hopes for winning." The mother realized she had an opportunity to discuss with their son the family, Christian pacifist view on war and consider a more appropriate response to the request. His rewritten card said: "We love you and hope you come back safely."

Several adults discovered a wide range of books that spoke to the subject of war and peace. In observance of Emergency Sabbath, just days following the outbreak of war, one adult read *The Sun and the Wind* (Newton: Faith and Life Press, 1983), an Aesop's fable rewritten by Cornelia Lehn, to the children at church. Two public schoolteachers found meaning with *Penguins of All People* by Don Freeman (New York: Viking, 1971) and *Here Comes the Cat* by Frank Asch and Vladimir Vagin (New York: Scholastic Books, 1989).

In the early 1960s, first-grader Ruby Bridges tried to attend school in New Orleans in spite of an angry mob harassing her. Robert Coles, author of *The Spiritual Life of Children* (Boston: Houghton Mifflin, 1990), was impressed that little Ruby's courage in facing her attackers was "rooted firmly in the biblical underpinnings of her faith," said book reviewer Arlice Davenport in *The Wichita Eagle* on January 27, 1991. "She was able to withstand such terrifying racial abuse by putting into practice a principle she had learned in Sunday school: Pray for those who persecute you; do good to those who hate you."

10. Share Belief Systems

During crisis, concentrate on belief systems that really matter to your family and talk about those with your children. "In our family, we believe . . ." are words that can help children balance what else they may hear from their friends and what may be happening in the community or the world. Help children understand the strength of being family and of sharing and cherishing peaceful responses to conflict and tension together.

A four-year-old was heard testing some family values with his grandpa while they watched television. "Are those the good guys or the bad guys?" he asked. And his grandpa wisely answered, "Those are good people, just doing the wrong thing."

"Love your enemies to pieces instead of shooting them to pieces," advised a five-year-old when her daddy asked.

A fourth-grade student wrote to a relative of her friend in the Middle East: "Have high hopes, high spirits, and you shall fly high. Have faith and dreams, and peace will soon come."

A nine-year-old in a peace activist family writes: "I can work for peace by wearing buttons on my coat, putting bumper stickers on our car, and going to demonstrations. I can also work for peace by telling others that war is wrong and telling them what peace is all about."

11. Pray with the Children

During the week of January 13, 1991, an Ohio congregation was in a week of Bible studies for all ages. For children who were together each day, the tensions in the Persian Gulf area became an experience of prayer and concern. They began with prayers that there not be war, then they asked God to help country leaders think twice before beginning war; they prayed that their country wouldn't shoot first. The children were devastated the night bombing started. They wept as they asked questions, shared their concerns, and prayed. There were hugs as they were comforted and assured of God's care and presence.

Two children of a peacemaking family are cared for by a sitter whose two sons serve in the military. These sons are regularly included in the children's bedtime prayers. They also pray that God will make the fighting stop and bring peace.

A six-year-old accompanied his father to a New Year's Eve peace vigil being held in a military park. The father wrote: "I think our son was really moved by the prayers, singing, candles. Almost before the observance was over, however, he and a friend eagerly ran off to play on the old Civil War cannons which are on display. It's frustrating to know that I cannot shield him from all of the violence there is in the world.

Viewing the World Through Global Perspectives

12. Stress Global Awareness

Children in the decade of the 1990s are aware of the world. Young school-age children can point out countries and cities on a globe around the world. Kuwait and Iraq and Saudia Arabia are household words.

A five-year-old announced: "I'm going on a vacation to Kuwait."

During pretend play a four and a five-year-old were driving a big truck into Iraq. But the bridge broke and the truck fell into the river.

And on the day the Persian Gulf War was declared over, a five-year-old was greatly relieved. "The war is finally over," he said. "They celebrated."

"Where?" asked the adult.

"In Kuwait," was his quick reply.

Indeed, children in peacemaking families share concerns for people around the world and are anxious about the plight of children in war-torn countries. Their awareness included a great deal of caring about others—a realization that interdependence throughout the world is a necessity.

A three-year-old and her mother were talking together before bedtime prayers. Their focus was on the children and other people who were hurt by the war, praying that somehow they could be happy again and that God would take away the sadness and anger that caused this war.

"Mommy, I don't think there are very many sad people in our country, but there are lots of sad people in other countries."

"Yeah, there are lots of sad people where the war is going on in other countries but that makes people in our country sad, too."

"But I think there are lots more sad people in other countries. Maybe I can share some of my marbles with them and that would make them happier. Do you think that's a good idea?" Just that day, the child had received a long-hoped-for bag of marbles which were extremely special.

A group of third graders in the classroom of a Christian pacifist teacher listed their dreams in chart form. Many of the concerns included global perspectives: make peace, end the world's pollution, end the war in the Middle East, stop killing endangered animals, stop oil spills, recycle and don't waste paper, save the rain forests, give equal rights to blacks and whites in South Africa, give freedom for everyone in the world.

A mother in a university city shared her global concerns in a letter to the principal of the school which her daughter attends. She asked, "When will we stop having children sing . . . a song that expresses the kind of nationalism that results in war between nations? Why not sing 'God Bless the Earth?' Instead of saying 'I pledge allegiance to the . . . U.S.A.,' why not 'I pledge allegiance to the Earth'?"

With global awareness, "each of us in the world is part of the others in the world. What happens to each one of us happens to the others of us. We must, therefore, stop thinking about life as some kind of contest to be won but as important work to be done together with our fellow human beings. . . . We must replace the idea of killing with the idea of living" (Sey Chassler in December 28, 1986, issue of *Parade* magazine).

Closing

At the beginning of 1990, a Sunday school class in the Midwest wrote promises for the new year and sealed them in an envelope. Later, children were invited to share their promises if they chose to do so. One child read his statement of hope for a world in crisis: "I promise never to kill anyone." Our hope for the world rests in affirmations such as that.

Teaching the young to trust in the care of nurturing adults around them, to live with hope in the God who sustains life, and to believe in themselves and their abilities to make a difference: those are the challenges for this moment and for all times.

Rosella Wiens Regier serves as executive director for the Anabaptist Curriculum Project for Children, with offices at General Conference Mennonite Church, Newton, Kansas. She has over twenty years of experience in public school and Christian education.

14
Empowering Teenagers for Peacemaking

Abe Bergen

We cannot wait for a war to break out before we begin to teach youth about peace and peacemaking. The foundation of our peace teaching must be established during times of peace and remain an ongoing concern of our educational agenda.

"Youth do not think about peace unless asked," commented John. "There is a general awareness and appreciation of the traditional peace stance but when it comes to specific applications, it falls short."

"Youth have ambiguous, untested convictions regarding peace," added Rachel. "We do very little teaching in our congregations, even though good resources are available. Educational credentials and financial security seem to be taking priority over peace convictions and service."

"The problem is that peace education efforts are inadequate and spotty. Present peace education resources do not connect with our youth. Much of our peace education has been narrowly focused on military conscription and nonpayment of war taxes which are only a part of the larger issues of peace and justice," lamented Norman.

In a Youth Peace Education Consultation held in Lagrange,

Illinois, in 1986, participants from the Mennonite Church and the General Conference Mennonite Church were asked about the status of peace convictions among youth. These comments reflected the perceptions of some of the youth leaders and peace educators who were present.

Similar perceptions were confirmed by the ongoing research of Search Institute. A Youth Research Survey taken in 1970 and updated in subsequent years found that only one of the five main preoccupations of youth resulted in a major shift: the voice of social conscience was not as loud and persistent in 1985 as in 1970. About one-third of church youth were concerned with social justice issues in 1970. That proportion was reduced to one-fifth in 1985 (Merton P. Strommen, *Five Cries of Youth*, San Francisco: Harper & Row, 1988).

Prior to the Peace Consultation, the reality of their country at war was not in the memory of most youth. There were seemingly no urgent reasons to discuss peace issues, especially those related to militarism and war. Given such a lack of interest, what strategies for peace education would effectively draw youth out of their lethargy? In the past, the threat of a military draft motivated youth to think through their own position on militarism and pacifism. With no immediate motivation, how could youth be interested in discussing issues of war and peace?

On January 16, 1991, the coalition forces declared war on Iraq. Our world will never be the same to the present generation of youth and children. For several days, children, youth, and adults became immobilized as their attention focused on the bombing of Baghdad. We received hour-by-hour, strike-by-strike accounts of what was happening nine time zones away. People around the world watched this "giant Nintendo game" in their living rooms.

During the weeks that followed, we remained riveted to our television screens, listening to endless analyses, detailed explanations of military strategies, and speculations about what to expect next as the war in the Persian Gulf unfolded. The nauseating rhetoric which justified the destruction of life and country was sickening.

In the face of this war, those who opposed it felt helpless and guilty. Politicians seemed determined to "resolve" this crisis with military might. The voices calling for diplomatic solutions fell on deaf ears. Persons committed to peace and nonviolence were plagued with guilt and remorse for not having worked harder to stop this war from happening. Prayer seemed like the only recourse in a world bent on destruction.

Many youth leaders recognized the importance of dealing with the harsh reality of death and destruction brought on by this war. Worship services, prayer vigils, and protest marches were organized on short notice to allow youth and adults alike to express their confusion, fears, and anger. These public events helped young people to voice the many emotions and thoughts which sought expression, reminded them that God was still their refuge and strength in times of distress, and allowed participants to support each other.

For many, the first month of the war was a time of grieving: grieving with the families who experienced the loss of loved ones; grieving for a people whose country and culture was rapidly being devastated by thousands of bombing missions; grieving for a world where the pride and egotism of a few world leaders sidelined all peaceful solutions; grieving for the young people throughout the world whose prejudice and hatred was fueled by the propaganda and events of this war.

Whether youth felt that this was a justified war or a senseless slaughter, all were deeply affected by the war. Peace was no longer an abstract idea or an irrelevant concern. It was impossible to remain neutral or apathetic about the happenings in the Persian Gulf. Sooner or later everyone was drawn into the heated discussions and debates about the issues of this war. Indifference was no longer possible.

In 1986, the interest and commitment to peacemaking among Mennonite youth had almost ground to a halt. To announce a discussion on peace at a youth event would assure low attendance or a least some groans. However, by mid-January 1991, the response had changed dramatically. For example, on Friday, January 19, several hundred students from Mennonite colleges and high schools in Manitoba converged on the legislative grounds in Winnipeg to demonstrate their concern for peace and listen to speakers share their viewpoints. Many youth spoke with conviction and passion. What was the difference?

The obvious answer was that we were involved in a war. Suddenly peace became a relevant concern for many. The war brought many emotions to the surface. Through newspaper articles, television coverage, and interviews on the radio, they became sad, angry, confused, discouraged, and frustrated about what they saw and heard. Young people had been affected on an emotional level which no longer permitted neutrality or disinterest. Apathy disappeared as the search for understanding the conflict and finding solutions to the war continued.

Feeling and Identifying

By reflecting on our response to the war in the Persian Gulf, we begin to understand some of the dynamics required for teaching peace to youth.

For most youth, the first step in a peace formation process is becoming involved on an emotional level, not just on an intellectual level. The war in the Persian Gulf generated an emotional response from youth. Issues of war and peace suddenly became relevant and thereby provided an opportunity to teach about peace.

From a Christian education point of view, we cannot wait for a war to break out before we begin to teach youth about peace and peacemaking. The foundation of our peace teaching must be established during times of peace and remain an ongoing concern of our educational agenda.

The absence of peace is usually a result of injustice. Individuals or groups often respond with violence when all other possibilities to rectify situations have been exhausted. In the Bible, peace and justice are closely linked. Biblical peace stands squarely against oppression and injustice and is central to biblical faith.

Many Mennonite youth are isolated and immunized from the injustices faced by people in their cities and the world beyond. Therefore they feel no urgency to work at changes which will bring about peaceful conditions. Many lack firsthand acquaintance with some of the pain and despair which is caused by discrimination on a personal or global scale. In order for youth to become involved in peacemaking, they must have experiences that evoke compassion and commitment to this biblical vision.

One way youth can become sensitized to the concern of others is by moving out of their safe, secluded environments and going to locations where they can observe life through the eyes of the oppressed. In the prologue to *Shalom: The Bible's Word for Salvation, Justice, and Peace*, Perry Yoder talks about spending four months in the Philippines and he describes how "shattering and shaping" his experiences were in this context of poverty, oppression, and struggle for change.

Likewise, if young people can be brought into situations where they can see for themselves how people suffer and talk personally with victims of inequality, they may be able to see life in new ways. Studying and analyzing cannot take the place of meeting victimized people face-to-face and listening to their stories. The idea of providing such experiences for youth is not new. The action/reflection model used in some education curriculums is based on this concept. The potential for linking justice and peace, motivating interest in peace issues, and deepening a commitment to peacemaking for youth can be exciting when they become directly involved in the issues.

Here is an example of one experiential encounter that was designed with the above objective in mind. In Winnipeg, an ad hoc committee developed an "urban plunge" experience with the explicit purpose of building bridges of understanding between Mennonite youth and people of the inner city. Groups of eight to fifteen would spend a weekend listening to stories of persons on welfare, serving in soup kitchens, and worshiping with an inner-city congregation on Sunday morning. In formal and informal ways they dialogued with residents of the inner city. It was hoped that after such an intentional experience, the youth would be able to see the world through new eyes, thereby breaking down the barriers of distance, fear, and prejudice.

Most participants had never seen Winnipeg from this vantage point. Their excursions to the city usually took them to malls, places of entertainment, or the suburbs. In this program, the youth listened to the hopes and dreams of inner-city residents and learned how poverty and circumstances repeatedly crushed their aspirations. They participated in evening gospel mission worship services and felt what it was like to sit through such a service as a prerequisite to their evening meal. Through simulation games led by people who were on social assistance, they experienced in small part the frustrations of a bureaucratic, inadequate welfare system.

When groups were able to come for a week rather than only a weekend, participants were placed within an agency or alongside someone who was responding to the everyday needs and hopes of the people living there. These included shelters for abused women, drop-in centers for street people, and community centers.

With few exceptions, the face-to-face encounters eroded stereotypes and prejudices. The people of the inner city were not all that different from the visiting youth. All shared similar dreams and aspirations, struggled with failures, and celebrated small successes. As the youth listened to the stories of the inner-city people, they were confronted with the fact that many opportunities the youth enjoyed were not available to these people of the inner city. It was not as simple as just telling poor people in the inner city to "pull themselves up by their bootstraps." Their stories of human triumph in spite of the obstacles inspired many of the youth.

Through the course of the weekend, participants in the "urban plunge" became more sensitive and compassionate. Some were challenged to pursue subsequent service opportunities, while others applied for a year or more of service through one of several voluntary service agencies. Regardless of long-term action responses, the memory of the faces of the people they met remained with them for some time. Consciously or unconsciously it became a point of reference from which to process further information. Interest in social issues and openness to further dialogue were immediate results.

Equally inspiring for the youth was meeting Christians involved in the work of peace and justice. Several members of the ad hoc planning group were residents in the area where the "plunge" took place. They had decided to live in solidarity with the residents in the inner city in order to get to know them, learn from them, and work together with them wherever possible. Their love for the people in their neighborhood was evident as they shared experiences of their encounters and helped the youth process their impressions and observations.

Meeting role models who intentionally chose to live here was inspiring for youth. They were impressed by the fact that these Christians were not here to "save" the inner city or the people who lived there, but had a sincere desire to live in solidarity with them. Over time they were able to build bridges of trust and friendship and become advocates for social justice.

Nurturing a compassionate awareness in youth begins when they become exposed to situations of injustice, when they listen to stories from victims of oppression, and when they interact with adults committed to ministries of justice and peacemaking. Such experiences impact youth on an emotional level and leave the door open for further reflection and action.

Learning and Understanding

After an empathetic bond is established, an important second step is to learn about the reasons for injustice. Arousing strong feelings in youth without channeling that energy further is a disservice to youth and the persons they have encountered. Open minds and hearts permit further analysis and teaching. One of the reflective exercises that generated a lot of discussion during an urban plunge was our "causes of poverty" discussion. A handout listing twelve causes of poverty was distributed to each individual. Students were asked to rank the three most powerful causes of poverty and to consider reasons for their ranking order. The next step invited them to share their ranking in a small group and attempt to agree on a ranking order by discussing their reasons within the group. In the third step, an effort was made to arrive at entire group consensus.

Seldom did groups agree on the main causes of poverty. However, the discussion broadened everyone's knowledge on this topic and thereby clearly reached the objective of this exercise. Identifying reasons—systemic, circumstantial, and personal—provided the information needed when considering further action. Once a problem is understood, the likelihood of choosing appropriate and purposeful action is much greater.

Solutions to difficult situations are usually complex and extensive. When a youth group becomes interested in a particular concern, it is appropriate to explore the issue in greater depth rather than consider it briefly on a superficial level and then move on to the next problem. If a long-term benefit is desired, a group may want to set aside a month or more to study the issue. The education process in a youth group should draw a theological connection to the discussion so that any action response which grows out of the study can be rooted in faith.

Imagining and Acting

Observing oppression and injustice results in grieving about present reality. Embracing this grief by naming the causes of inequality invites consideration of new possibilities for the future. Finally, there is readiness to talk about what can be changed to address the present shortcomings and create a more hopeful future for all.

Our imaginations contribute to creating a vision for the future. In *The Bible Makes Sense*, Walter Brueggemann writes about the importance of nurturing a "historical imagination." Imagination alone tends to become undisciplined fantasy and might move us in haphazard directions. Historical awareness without imagination becomes arid and uncompelling. Together, they bring newness and vitality.

The involvement of youth in helping to create a future vision is important for two reasons. First, youth are often full of idealistic fervor and free from traditional blinders. This places them in a position to develop creative alternatives to present realities. Second, if action is to grow out of this new vision, it is necessary for them to own the vision by helping to shape it.

A youth/adult partnership contributes to a more durable vision as it ensures that the imaginative is also grounded in the historical and particular. Furthermore, adults can assist youth with the translation of ideas into reality. By using their experience and skills, they can empower youth to make a difference.

Genuine concern is best expressed in action. Action leads to further reflection, growth, and often more action. This was illustrated in an article published in a teen magazine. Jon Zimmerman, a young adult from Lancaster, Pennsylvania, reflects on a three-and-a half-week service assignment in Kenya with STAT—Summer Training Action Teams: "I came away from Kenya with a strong desire to go into long-term missions later on. That wasn't a new idea, but I now have a much stronger sense of call in that direction. I suppose that has to do a lot with the fact that no longer is service something I do just out of a sense of duty; now it's my grateful response to a Friend who cares about me. . ." (*With*, March 1991).

Peacemaking includes building bridges of understanding, encouraging reconciliation between people, and addressing the causes of injustice and oppression. Often youth (and adults) must be taken out of their comfortable situations and placed in new settings before their eyes will be opened and their hearts warmed to the realities around them. Once an emotional connection is made, the motivation to become involved in peacemaking is kindled.

While the interest in peacemaking has decreased in our youth, the good news is that at least one-fifth of our youth are bright, aware, change-oriented persons who are sensitive to other people and desperately want to make this world a better place. If the compassion of these youth can be evoked, if they can be brought to a deeper understanding of the factors which prevent peace, and if they can be assisted in using their giftedness to make a difference, they will be able to draw in other youth and become peacemakers in our world.

Postscript

I am adding these paragraphs on February 28, the day after a cease-fire was declared in the Persian Gulf. While many people felt this war was senseless and unnecessary, I am aware that it took place because a majority in Canada, the United States, and other coalition countries wanted it to proceed. We were told time and again that it was a just war and that we had a moral obligation to resolve the crisis through war. Because we came to accept this line of thinking, we permitted our politicians to wage war.

I became more aware than ever how rhetoric prepares us to accept and justify war. The media was used extensively to control our thinking. Iraqis were portrayed as evil villains who needed to be taught a lesson. Yet when we think of the fewer than 100 casualties on the side of the coalition forces and the tens or even hundreds of thousands of casualties on the Iraqi side, who perpetuated the greater evil? Some justified the actions of the coalition forces, including the bombing civilian targets and retreating armies, because these were the bad guys.

To a great extent, the media controlled what we were shown and told. Those who believed the propaganda became champions and defenders of this war. If youth and adults in the Christian churches of Canada and the United States had been committed to peace, and had critiqued the war rhetoric from that commitment, this war could not have happened. Therefore it is urgent that we intensify our commitment to teach the principles of peace and peacemaking to the youth of our churches, lest we forget the lessons of this war.

Abe Bergen, Winnipeg, Manitoba, serves as the secretary for youth education for the General Conference Mennonite Church. He also teaches courses in youth ministry at Canadian Mennonite Bible College. He holds a doctorate in ministry from Bethany Theological Seminary.

15
Young Adults and War: The Burdening of a Generation

Randy Keeler

Is someone willing to challenge young adults to respond [to issues of peace and justice] the way Christ would respond, or are his teachings too idealistic and archaic for the real world?

His school jacket with its neatly sewn varsity letter has been stored away in the hall closet. The picture of the young couple at the senior social is on the living room mantle. Next to it, his senior picture portrays an innocence untouched by the outside world. A few trophies finish the memorial to youthful days gone by.

For now the varsity letter has been exchanged for combat fatigues and infantryman's gear. The young woman standing next to him at the senior social waits patiently at home. The boyish senior picture has been replaced by an image of a young man in military uniform. Today he is learning combat maneuvers in some Middle Eastern desert, and the days of high school seem long removed.

At the height of the Persian Gulf conflict, these images were depicted almost daily by the news media. The visual images were usually accompanied by the voice of a mother reading a letter in which her son poured out his soul about the life and death situations he faced daily. Emotion cracked her voice; she wiped away a tear. Sympathy for families abounded from every viewing household. Viewers asked themselves how they would feel if that was their son, their daughter, their brother, or their friend over in the desert.

Conflicting Values

Support of the Gulf War by an overwhelming majority of North Americans has been surprising. College campuses hosted rallies—not to voice protests reminiscent of the 1960s, but to show support for the troops. Young executives in the city wear "support the troops" pins, and yellow ribbons adorn their offices and car antennas. In some communities, national and "we support our troops" flags wave in the wind outside so many households that every day seems like a national holiday. The young adults of the land, not having lived through any previous wars, believe the support to be normal and expected.

This generation of young adults has grown up on media role models like Rambo, Superman, Rocky, and Ghostbusters. If someone messes with us, how have we been taught to respond? There is no other alternative but to blast them, mess 'em up, or waste them. And while we take care of the evil intruder, despite overwhelming odds and despite the incredible threat to our own lives, we will somehow come out of it all amazingly unscathed— maybe a little dirty, but we'll surely be around for the sequel. As the military personnel sat waiting in the desert, there were some who obviously were already negotiating their contract for the sequel by saying things like, "I just want to get the job done and get out of here." Rambo would have been proud.

Media support for the war was convincing to younger people. Daily, the public was shown bombing missions that resembled video games. It was made to look so easy—like pushing the button on a joystick, guiding the projectile to its destination, hitting the target and receiving the highest possible total of points. For some reason, we've been convinced that all those bombs being dropped did not involve people, but just military targets. Enemy military personnel were portrayed as something less than human. Media stories about pacifists and peacemakers depicted the subjects as idealistic or archaic.

Churches across the land were shown supporting the war and the troops. Communitywide church services supported the war and the troops from their particular communities. We have been told that a leading evangelical preacher gave his blessing to President Bush for the war to begin.

All of these factors which influence and shape the lives of the young adults around us, make the task of passing on the church's deeply held convictions regarding peace more difficult. Just as the Christian faith is always one generation away from extinction, even more so is the peace doctrine of the church. Churches who have been consistent through the years in their peace teachings have weathered Desert Storm fairly well. These church's young people, although questioning for themselves what they believe, have shown the ability to see through the media hype and ask questions consistent with the Anabaptist concerns for peace.

Some churches in the peace church tradition have resisted teaching about peace. They cite reasons of church growth—not wanting to offend the newcomer to the fellowship from another faith tradition. In their silence, these churches have been endorsing the militaristic attitudes in the community around them. As a result, the young adults in these churches are struggling now as the church leadership brings the peace doctrine of the church "out of the closet."

Some churches have continued to resist teaching about peace during this time so as not to offend anyone, which calls the integrity of the pulpit into question. If the Word of God does not touch life issues now in the midst of a worldwide crisis, does it ever really touch our lives? Young adults are ready to hear what the church leadership has to say about the world situation, but instead they are often led in a general prayer which takes no position. Is someone willing to challenge young adults to respond the way Christ would respond, or are his teachings too idealistic and archaic for the real world?

The Young Adult Search for Faith

Don, a nineteen-year-old Mennonite youth, had been having problems finding a job since his high school graduation a year earlier. Don made a decision to follow Christ during his junior high years, but in high school he drifted somewhat from the church and was viewed as rebellious by the rest of the youth group. When he brought his friends to church activities they often smelled of smoke and alcohol.

I remember Don as a camper, at our church camp, who always wore army fatigues when we played our weekly capture-the-flag campwide game. He carried a utility knife and seemed to love the adventure of the out-of-doors. Somehow it did not surprise me when I learned that Don had joined the army, despite the pacifist leanings of his father.

Soon after entering the military, Don recommitted his life to the Lord at a military chapel service. Although his parents would not have wished for Don to enter the military, how does the church respond to a family situation in which the parents are happy that their son has at least made a deeper faith commitment, regardless of this belief in peace? Even though the church's view would be that military service is wrong, was it right for Don?

Brian is an eighteen-year-old high school honors student and a member of a Mennonite church. His plans after graduation included studying engineering at a prestigious school. He took the entrance tests and was accepted into the program. On a service project with his youth group immediately preceding his senior year in high school, Brian recommitted his life to God. Now he is talking about spending a year in missions before pursuing any undergraduate studies. His strong peace convictions as a result of his renewed faith commitment have caused him to write letters to the editor of the local newspaper and to speak as a resource in group settings to other non-Mennonite youth groups.

The faith stories of Don and Brian demonstrate to us that the experience of faith is different for every individual. The context of Don's significant faith experience was in a setting where peaceful solution to conflict was not upheld as an ideal. Until Don is removed from his present situation, it may be difficult for him to see a different point of view, although some people do leave the military as conscientious objectors after having a significant faith experience during their time of active duty. Brian's context for recommitment helped to affirm the peace convictions which were being taught consistently in his congregation. His expression of strong peace convictions was part of his larger expression of a renewed faith.

Lavon Welty, in his book, *Blueprint for Congregational Youth Ministry* (Faith and Life Press and Mennonite Publishing House, 1989), has identified "the search for significance" as the theme which dominates the life of young people during late adolescence. According to Welty, significance is "a basic attitude or orientation toward oneself . . . significance is confirmed when others affirm the capabilities and accomplishments of a person" (page 22). At the point where an individual is involved in an activity that is viewed as significant, or where an individual is treated as a significant person, that individual will direct his or her activities in the direction from which the affirmation is coming.

In *Young Adult Ministry*, Terry Hershey characterizes the eighteen- to twenty-two-year-old age range as a time of "pulling up roots." It is during this time that individuals seek for something significant on which to build their identity. That something may be a peer group, a hero or role model, an ideology, or a cause.

Both Don and Brian, in the midst of their having found significance, chose a higher level of faith commitment. In each case, the Christian community was close by to help them make the connection between life and faith. In light of this fact, can the church claim to be a place where young adults find the significance for which they long, and make the connection between life and faith?

Just at the time that young adulthood is reached, significant decisions regarding life and faith have to be made. Vocational choice is, of course, at the forefront of their thinking. Should I go to college? Should I find a job in the community? If I choose to go to college, how will I pay for it? Is serving in the military an option to help pay for my education? What opportunities does the church present to me for missions and service? Does being a Christian impact any of my decisions?

Many young adults are fearful that a draft is in the near future because of the intensity of the world situation. Is the church ready to accept the fact that its young people will make decisions based on where they have sensed a recognition of their significance? The church now has an exciting opportunity to share its unique peacemaking convictions with its young adult members. The time is ripe. They are now willing to listen.

The Church's Role in Young Adult Faith Development

To say that the church has a role in faith development is an understatement, and the task of this essay is not to outline the full scope of that role. However, there are some significant things that the church can be doing to help its young people understand how peacemaking and faith are part of the larger life and faith question.

1. *Biblical Teaching.* If a congregation has been lax in its teachings on peace, now is the time to find an appropriate context

where teaching can happen. Young adults will respond to good, coherent, biblical teaching on peace. Many of them are tired of the debates over political questions. What does the Scripture say that can help them provide a context upon which to build their political opinions? This could happen in a young adult Sunday school class, midweek Bible study, sermon series, or one-on-one discipling. One church conference has provided conferencewide events for youth and young adults in the way of seminars, Bible studies, and retreats which specifically address the biblical perspectives on the Persian Gulf conflict. The response has been overwhelming.

2. *Stories of Conscientious Objectors.* Most congregations and all church conferences have members who proclaimed themselves as conscientious objectors in the past and who would be more than willing to share their stories. Provide a time during a morning worship service where these persons could share their faith stories. Young adults want to see some flesh put on the doctrine. Who in the church has lived out these beliefs to the point where it really affected his or her life? A former army tank commander with six years of military experience was given an opportunity to share his faith story. When the young adults present heard of how Jesus made a significant impact on this tank commander's life—to the point of his claiming conscientious objector status even during peacetime—something spiritual really moved in the room. He had their full attention. This former tank commander is now a Mennonite pastor.

3. *Become Informed of Conscientious Objector Legal Questions.* Young adults need assistance in sorting through the legal questions and processes regarding obtaining conscientious objector status. Even though draft registration in the United States does not directly affect those of us who are past legal draft age, we need to take it upon ourselves to keep informed about the draft laws which could affect our young adults. Each congregation within the peace church tradition should commit itself to finding at least one adult who is willing to keep current on the draft laws and pass that information on to the rest of the congregation. One church conference has made an attempt to appoint at least one person in each of its congregations who is willing to fulfill this task. The conference youth minister then periodically brings current issues to their attention through mailings or meetings.

4. *Recruit Young Adults for Service in God's Kingdom.* The church needs to be doing more than just discouraging young adults from

military service. The church needs to also be encouraging young
adults towards Christian service. The military recruiting adver-
tisements depict their service as full of adventure. Young people
are told that if they serve in the military they will be doing
something significant for both their country and for themselves.
A young person with a good academic record and extracurricular
involvement is recruited heavily by the military. One son of a
Mennonite pastor received eighteen calls in his senior year from
the same navy recruiter. Do we recruit our young people with the
same zeal that military recruiters do? Do we encourage our
young people to do something significant for the church and for
their own future by committing a period of their lives to voluntary service in God's kingdom? Some congregations have ap-
pointed a person for this very purpose. This designated person is
kept informed as to the various service opportunities which the
church has to offer.

5. *Deal Pastorally with Those Who Choose the Military.* The peace
churches in general have not had a good record of relating to
young adults redemptively when they return from active military
duty. The church has generally responded in two ways: forcing
immediate repentance, which in many cases has resulted in a
drawing away by the young adult; and the other extreme, an
open acceptance of the person without any form of contact from
the pastor helping them to explore the meaning of their time of
military service and how it relates to the larger issue of faith
experience. Somehow the church has to deal pastorally with its
young men and women who return from military duty. They
need to feel accepted, yet to be encouraged to continue to grow in
their understanding of Jesus' gospel of peace. As adults in the
congregation continue to strive towards greater faithfulness in
Christ, an important part of that goal should be to make sense of
how Jesus' message of peace is lived out in a violent world. If the
leadership approaches this issue with the realization that each
member of the body of Christ is continually in process towards
greater faithfulness, it invites young adults to accept the challenge of also growing in their understanding of a sincere, lived
faith. This is an issue in which we are truly called to hate the sin,
but love the sinner.

Hope for the Continuing Vision

To see so many young adults affirm the peace teachings of Jesus
Christ has truly been an inspiration for those adults who have

wondered if biblical peacemaking will survive another generation. These contemporary conscientious objectors need to be held high in the faith and made to realize the significant impact they are having in the ongoing life of the church.

Instead of the motto being "support our troops," can the motto now read "support our peacemakers"? Can the church raise the level of awareness of conscientious objection to the point where significance can be found in taking a stand against the status quo in the world around them? Will young adults who take this stand be supported by the community of faith?

The task of peacemaking should not be brought to bear alone on the young adults of this generation. Believers of all ages should assume the responsibility of sharing the message of peacemaking with younger believers and with people in the world around them.

Randy Keeler is a minister with youth and young adults in the Eastern District Conference of the General Conference Mennonite Church and the Franconia Conference of the Mennonite Church.

16

Five Congregations Respond to Conflict

Sometimes I wonder, is praying all we can do? Then I . . . was reminded that prayer is really the most important work that we as God's people can do.

Laura J. Loewen

When I was asked to write how our congregation, the Mennonite Fellowship of Montreal, had responded to the summer 1990 conflict between native Canadians and law enforcement officials at Oka, Quebec, and how we responded to the Middle East conflict, I cringed a little. What, indeed, had we done or are we doing. Certainly nothing very earthshaking!

The crisis at Oka was a concern for us. We talked about it and prayed. The local churches' hands seemed to be tied because there wasn't any good link to the communities at either Kahnawake or Kahnesetake. Slowly, some contacts with these communities were established. Our congregation was invited to participate in prayer vigils. Some of us attended. We were invited to be observers at strategic points along the reserve (reservation). Eight persons from our congregation spent one glorious sunny day in the fresh air keeping track of ingoing and outgoing vehicles. Was there really any significance to this activity? Would we have been as willing to go on a rainy day? These were questions we asked ourselves after a long day of very little action.

Our news programs continued to show angry confrontations between the native community and the "outside" world. Were there no other more positive images that could be flashed across the country? Out of this concern came the idea that perhaps if a group from the Mennonite church met with a group of native Canadians at one of the barricades and sang peace songs to each other, the country might also see images of bridge building taking place between the two races.

The hymn-sing did not proceed as planned. We were met at the barricades by some very angry local residents (not native Canadians). We did sing one song and prayed, but then we left. Our intentions to bring overtures of peace to one group had antagonized another group. We didn't question our intentions, but we did question the wisdom of this action. We went home and continued praying for the people caught in this crisis.

Several months later we invited several people from Oka to share their side of the story with us. Hearing their story was helpful. It was also very encouraging to hear that the churches' prayer vigils and network of observers had given the native community hope. Perhaps our participation in these peace efforts was not as insignificant as we had assumed.

These days our congregation is praying about another crisis, the one in the Middle East. A weekly prayer vigil was begun shortly after Christmas, and we decided to continue this vigil on a weekly basis at least until Easter. As we shared, sang, and prayed, we were reminded that the Middle East is at our doorstep. Our Arab and Jewish brothers and sisters in Montreal are in pain because of what has taken place in the Persian Gulf. We asked ourselves whether there was some way in which we as a Mennonite group could begin to build some bridges to these two communities. One way, we thought, would be for us to hear their stories and for them to hear that we want to extend our hands in friendship. We don't know what our next step will be, but in the meantime, we will continue praying.

Praying together as a group has been a meaningful experience. Sometimes I wonder, is praying *all* we can do? Then I read "Sentences on Peacemaking" by Henri Nouwen and was reminded that prayer is really the most important work that we as God's people can do. I would like to share several of these thoughts:

Prayer—living in the presence of God—is the most radical

peace action we can imagine. Prayer *is* peacemaking and not simply the preparation before, the support during, and the thanksgiving after.

Prayer is not primarily a way to get something done. In prayer we undo the fear of death and therefore the basis of all human destruction.

. . . the act of prayer is the basis and source of all action. When our actions against the arms race are not based on the act of prayer, they easily become fearful, fanatical, bitter, and more of an expression of survival instincts than of our faith in God and the God of the living (*Seeds of Hope*, Henri Nouwen, Bantam, 1989).

As I write this I am also very aware of the continuing struggle that exists in Quebec—a struggle that continues to bring division in our own country. Can we find ways of being peacemakers in this context? I pray that we will.

Laura J. Loewen is pastor of the Mennonite fellowship of Montreal.

We have felt tension and testing, but the result has been growth.

Tim Schrag

Finding ways to respond to the crisis in the Middle East has been good for our congregation. We have felt tension and testing, but the result has been growth.

We responded in various ways through our worship experiences. In September 1990 I preached two sermons on themes related to the impending war. The first was on having the mind of Christ, and in the second we explored the Old Testament and war.

As a congregation, we met one evening last fall to pray, discuss our feelings about the military buildup in the Persian Gulf region, and to listen to each others' views.

In the weeks since the middle of January, several more sermons have focused on the conflict, including one after the cease-fire. This sermon suggested that we should not be euphoric over the military victory, but that we should focus our energy on compassion and relief efforts.

A church member submitted the "Open Letter to the Iraqi People," which had been published in the *Mennonite Weekly Review,* to our local newspaper. To our surprise, the paper reprinted this letter, in its entirety, in the editorial slot.

Since the crisis began, we have put into motion more energetic and intentional plans to guide youth in their understanding of the Mennonite peace position. As part of this, our district conference youth worker held a draft-counseling session with the youth.

Many of our actions have been internal, that is, they took place within our congregation. We have been reluctant to be more visible and active in our witness to the community.

One reason for this reluctance is theological uncertainty. We are not clear as a congregation as to whether we should take an activist peacemaking stance or the more traditional two-kingdom stance. We do not agree among ourselves about witnessing to the government.

Another reason for lack of public witness was practical—those favoring more action could not agree on what to do in a visible way, so we did nothing.

The third reason was simply fear. We are a small, relatively isolated island of Mennonites in a sea of patriotic, generally hawkish neighbors. Since World War II we have gradually gained acceptance and respect as mainstream community members. Some church members fear that witness against war would sabotage these gains. Not everyone feels this fear to the same degree; some do not feel it at all. But it is a factor in our decision making.

Tim Schrag is the pastor of First Mennonite Church, Beatrice, Nebraska.

*We are confident that prayer is the most
effective weapon we can use for peace.*

Adam Liu

Our congregation holds a prayer meeting every Saturday morning at six. During the last three months, the first thing we prayed for was peace in the Persian Gulf. We prayed that the war could be avoided, but it happened. The Sunday after the war broke out, during our worship service, I asked our congregation to kneel and offer a prayer for peace in the Persian Gulf.

We deeply committed ourselves to prayer regarding this conflict, because we are confident that prayer is the most effective weapon we can use for peace. As we read in Daniel 10:13, we believe that the "prince of the kingdom of Persia"—Satan—is still controlling the Persian Gulf and even the whole universe. During the eight years of the conflict between Iraq and Iran, one million innocent people died, as if to tell the world, "life is worthless, it has only the value of an ant." This is clearly against the will of the Creator. We prayed that neither George Bush nor Saddam Hussein might be deceived by this evil power.

In "An Offering of Slogans," William Willimon, chaplain at Duke University, says that "peace is something God makes—a gift of God, not our enlightened social policy." He makes the point that "peace is not the fruit of our work for justice, ironically, violence is usually the result of our efforts to make peace," and goes on to say that the slogan " 'If you want peace, work for justice' reflects Christian accommodation to the agenda of idealogies that are not Christian." Willimon continues, "Contrary to notions prevalent in today's heavily politicized church, our task is not to be useful within the present scheme of things, but to be faithful. Modern people value power above all else, power to change the world, joining our hands to set things right. But setting things right, in itself, is not the supreme moral action. The supreme moral action, from a peculiarly Christian perspective, is to live and die as Christ."

I believe more and more people will be recognizing the true biblical way of peace. I am excited to know that the United Nations Commission on Human Rights declared in 1987 that conscientious objection to war is a basic human right.

In speaking about Jesus' nonviolence, Helmut Harder gives this solid conclusion: "[Jesus] chose to reconcile rather than to retaliate and he taught the same way to his disciples. This surely applies to all disciples in all generations and to all who claim the priority of the kingdom of heaven over all other loyalties."

Adam Liu is pastor of the Santa Clara Mennonite Church, Santa Clara, California.

We engaged in these efforts as a way to testify to our belief in the teachings of Jesus.

Alan Moore-Beitler

The war in the Persian Gulf exposed a range of deep feelings and emotions in our congregation. Anger, sadness, frustration, feelings of despair and powerlessness, serious questions about the real nature and depth of our own commitment to peace and pacifism all came rushing to the surface from the days of December preceding the war through January and February.

The invitation to write down the range of responses individuals and the congregation have made to this crisis also brought another emotion to me—hope. And that, I realized, had been in rather short supply through those days.

My hope was sparked as I realized how much we have done to find ways to give voice to our concerns and fears, as well as our commitment to strive to be peacemakers and followers of Jesus. Our congregation responded to the war in three areas: worship, education, and witness.

Our corporate worship was shaped by:

• **Prayer.** Each Sunday since early December we prayed about the crisis. During our Wednesday evening Advent gatherings, prayers about the impending war were also offered.

• **Fasting.** In response to an initiative proposed by leaders of the Mennonite and General Conference churches, various members participated in a one-day fast for peace on December 16.

• **Symbol.** With the outbreak of hostilities on January 16, the following Sunday and for each Sunday until the war was over we lit a solitary candle on the organ. This candle for peace symbolized our desire for peace and our commitment to pray and act for peace.

• **Confession.** Sunday, January 20, was an unusual worship experience. People needed to express their concerns and prayers about the war. The response was overwhelming. For forty-five minutes people spoke movingly about their feelings. There was a range and diversity of opinions expressed, but not in a sense of debate, rather in a spirit of confession. It was a very powerful, moving service.

• **Interfaith Prayer Service.** I was asked to help organize an interfaith prayer service for peace that took place in early February at the neighboring Methodist church. One of our members sang "The Prayer of St. Francis" as a solo.

We responded to the war through education:

• **Legislative Contacts.** Persons were encouraged to phone the White House, their senators, and congresspersons to express their views. A number of people sent letters to the president and members of Congress.

• **Petition.** In mid-December we drafted a petition expressing the Christian basis for our opposition to the military buildup and the growing potential for war, and requested that peaceful means be used to resolve this situation. Nearly fifty signatures were obtained. This was sent to appropriate members of Congress, the president, and the secretary of state.

• **Lenten Study Series.** Following the worship service on January 20, the pastorate (elders) wondered if a special series of meetings to further probe our feelings and questions about this conflict would interest people. It did. An outside resource person with seminary teaching experience was contacted and a five-week Lenten series was held on Sunday evenings. Attendance was exceptional.

• **Adult Sunday School.** In addition to providing the evening Lenten series, the adult education committee committed two Sunday morning class sessions to talking about the war. This was done to benefit those who were unable to attend the evening series and was designed to be focused on more personal sharing of struggles and questions the war raised.

• **Writing.** A member of our congregation submitted some of her personal journal writings to a denominational magazine. Though her prayers and struggles with the war were personal, she felt led to offer them in this way for others to read and reflect upon.

Members of the congregation also engaged in witness:

• **Sojourners/Pax Christi Candlelight March and All-Night Prayer Vigil.** A number of members of our congregation gathered at the National Cathedral on Monday evening, January 14. Following a brief service of singing and prayers, a candlelight march of three miles to the White House was held. This was followed by an all-night prayer vigil at a downtown church.

• **Civil Disobedience.** Four members of the congregation were joined by a Catholic woman in an act of prayerful civil disobedience on Tuesday, January 15, outside the White House. Surrounded by other members of the congregation for support, this witness was intended to express our conviction that although the United Nations was now approving violent force in Kuwait, we were calling for another way—the way of nonviolent love.

• **Public Demonstrations.** National marches opposing the war were held in Washington on January 19 and 26. Persons from our congregation attended both of these rallies. We also provided overnight hospitality at our church for a group of students from Bluffton (Ohio) College who drove out for the rally on January 26. Several persons also opened up their homes that weekend for people who came to the march.

• **CPT Emergency Sabbath.** Following an initiative proposed by Christian Peacemaker Teams, the congregation was invited to take an emergency Sabbath from work for one day to visit members of Congress and hold a public vigil for peace. Though turnout was light for this event, it was held on Tuesday, January 22.

• **Campus Organizing.** Two attenders of the church who are graduate students at nearby University of Maryland were involved in actions for peace on that campus. Interfaith Silent Vigils for Peace were organized and held on Wednesdays throughout the crisis. Additionally, a Middle East Peace Committee arranged regular rallies and a march, calling for an end to the war, through the College Park campus.

• **Peace Sign.** A member of the church proposed a sign expressing our concerns for peace be placed out front by a busy four-lane highway. This suggestion had made its way through levels of congregational decision making and was about to be constructed when the war ended.

By way of conclusion I would say members of our congregation engaged in all these efforts as a way to testify to our belief in the teachings of Jesus. These efforts also helped express our desire to respond in some ways, however seemingly small, to a war that cost thousands of human lives, a war that tragically seems to have bolstered our nation's commitment to militarism into the next decade and century.

Alan Moore-Beitler is pastor of the Hyattsville Mennonite Church, Hyattsville, Maryland.

The crisis in the Middle East and the war that came out of it have been a heavy burden for us as we have tried to find Christlike ways to respond.

Henry Krause

How do we respond to evil? to war, death, and destruction? Responding as peacemakers is not easy, especially when the war is seen as moral and God-ordained by many people.

Ours is a small congregation of around seventy people. We have tried through the dozen years of our existence to do peacemaking and reconciliation, and that has been a central focus of our work as a fellowship. We have tried to make the good news of Jesus real in a hurting world.

The crisis in the Middle East and the war that came out of it have been a heavy burden for us as we have tried to find Christlike ways to respond. Some of our members have close ties with the United States, and so even though we are a Canadian congregation, there is also the added dimension of not only our own national involvement, but also the connections with U.S. foreign policy.

One of our members has a sister and brother-in-law who are missionaries in Jordan, and who left for their reassignment in October of 1990 knowing that they were going back into a volatile situation—but also knowing that it was their calling from God. Although they are not from our fellowship, this connection has made the conflict much more real for us.

Our church tried to respond to the crisis in the Gulf in a number of ways. We participated in the oil-free Sunday in October sponsored by the Christian Peacemaker Teams. Some of our members walked to a local church or used fewer vehicles as a way of drawing attention to our overconsumption of oil.

In December we encouraged our members to write Christmas cards of peace to our prime minister and members of parliament, to greet them in the name of the Prince of Peace and also encourage them to take Jesus' words about loving enemies seriously.

We have a time of sharing every Sunday morning during our worship service and have consistently raised the issue of the Gulf War and the need to pray for victims, soldiers, and families during this time.

Our Community Concerns Committee drafted letters to our prime minister and others urging them to seek peaceful solutions to the conflict. These were made available for people to sign or to use as models for their own letters.

The Monday after war broke out, we had an Evening of Peace for the Middle East. We put articles in the local paper inviting the community to join us in a vigil of prayer, music, and silence. Reporters from our local paper participated in the vigil and covered the evening service in the paper. Our focus was threefold. First, to reaffirm that God is our source of life, hope, and salvation; secondly, to see the enemy as real people—women, children, families—and to somehow put faces to the enemy. We were helped to do this by one of our members who had spent time in the Middle East. He passed around photos of friends he had made there, told us who they were and some things about them.

Another focus was to realize that our response needed to be one of standing alongside victims of this war. These victims include civilians, soldiers, and families of those who were in the conflict. Our calling as Christians is to be present in the midst of suffering.

We lit candles, and used maps, posters, and photos to draw attention to the reality of the destruction and death of the war. We have continued to keep ourselves informed through the information that is being published by Mennonite Central Committee and Christian Peacemaker Teams. We are using these materials as a way of building in solidarity with many other Christians. This is helping us realize that we are not alone, but working together as a larger community of people trying to be faithful.

Our goal was to open our events to the public, so that our responses could be a witness to the truth about this gospel we believe. This has been a way to carry on the work of evangelism amid our feelings of frustration and uncertainty about what was happening in the world. It has been a good opportunity to say to the community that the church, and specifically the Mennonite church, stands in a long tradition of saying NO to evil and war, and YES to love and peacemaking—for this is the true calling of the church.

Henry Krause is pastor of the Langley Mennonite Fellowship, Langley, British Columbia.

17
When Faith Comes Under Fire

Katie Funk Wiebe

What keeps the vision of Christ's love for one's enemy from dimming when faith is under the fire of sometimes unanswerable questions?

Bonaparte, the young Irish soldier in Frank O'Connor's *Guests of the Nation*, wasn't told to keep his distance from the two English prisoners he and two other Irish soldiers were guarding in a small cottage near a woods. So he and another inexperienced guard played cards, argued at length about religion and politics, and attended local dances with the Englishmen. Enemies became friends.

Suddenly the order came to shoot the prisoners because the English had shot some Irish prisoners. The youthful Bonaparte was distraught. He argued: You don't kill a pal. But the military order said he had to.

An older guard, who had remained aloof from the Britishers, determindedly led the dark way to the woods, where with nothing but "a patch of lantern-light" and "birds hooting and screeching all round, disturbed by the guns," he shot the two blindfolded Englishmen. When one man was not killed outright, Bonaparte, out of pity, put his own gun to his friend's temple and ended his suffering.

He returned to the cottage in shock: "I was somehow very

small and very lost and lonely like a child astray in the snow. And anything that happened to me afterwards, I never felt the same about again." He moved from innocence to awareness about the violence of war.

Lost and lonely like a child astray in the snow. These words describe some people when they realized they weren't watching a Western-style movie the evening Desert Storm began. No good guys in white hats stalked bad guys in black ones to a certain victory.

Fighting on Many Fronts

William M. Mason wrote in the *Wichita Eagle* (Public Opinion, February 4, 1991) of his intense loneliness as a twenty-eight-year-old male when the Persian Gulf killing began. "I feel alone. My wife, my son, my work—nothing can drive away the emptiness I have experienced these last few weeks. I question my task on this planet, my value, my ability to encourage my son to go out into the world and make a difference. I feel alone on the planet where my brothers and sisters in this human family don't know me and I don't know them."

Any war is always fought on many fronts. Alongside the military battle is a political battle, sometimes aided and sometimes hindered by the media. We watch a media-managed war. People also fight a battle of conscience and of the soul to maintain faith. Now, suddenly, they are forced to re-sort convictions in the light of current events and be counted. And it isn't easy. Especially if they stand alone. The workplace is aflutter with yellow ribbons and flags. Co-workers are ready to argue patriotism at the drop of a paper clip.

Peace versus justice is a dilemma for the nonviolent Christian. The temporary successful use of violence makes it difficult for the voice of peace to speak clearly. Difficult questions assault those who lean even slightly toward an anti-war stance: Aren't you socially irresponsible if you allow rampant evil to go unchecked? There is only one way to stop madmen like Hitler and Saddam Hussein—by killing them. How can you allow other men and women to sacrifice their lives so that you can live in peace and comfort? Where's your patriotism?

What keeps the vision of Christ's love for one's enemy from dimming when faith is under the fire of sometimes unanswerable questions?

Clearly, a nation at war is not a time for pacifist triumphalism even though the number of conscientious objectors (for varied reasons) is larger than in previous wars. Open military conflict is always a time for inner searching for light and humility to allow the Spirit of Christ to shine forth. The carnage of war has no glory though an array of ribbons cover uniforms and medals blind the eyes. Nonviolence has no glory either unless it reflects the Spirit of Christ.

When a house catches on fire, residents quickly grab for valued possessions. In the crisis of war and its aftermath, what sustains us and makes our witness effective as members of the kingdom of the Spirit?

Faithfulness Renewed Through Conflict

Risk everything to maintain inner peace. Draw it to your heart. Cherish it. Nurture it. The assurance of peace with God through our Lord Jesus Christ is the basis of all. Many peace activists dropped their cause during the Vietnam era because it had no central core of strength. "Peace I leave with you; my peace I give you. I do not give to you as the world gives. Do not let your hearts be troubled and do not be afraid," Jesus told his disciples (John 14:27).

Anxiety about war progress drains energies, fears about the well-being of military personnel and civilians (collateral damage) depress waking hours, and tension about what may come after the fighting stops disturbs sleep. These human feelings of sorrow, fear, and depression are the real parts of our lives in the world, but "when we are freed from them—however briefly—by the peace the world cannot give, then we know a different kind of reality," writes Barbara Brown Taylor (*Weavings*, March/April 1988). "For he himself is our peace," Paul wrote to the Ephesians (2:14). Christ reconciled us to God through the cross of Christ. Cling to this reality of life.

Conflict of any kind is always an opportunity for the renewal of faith in Christ and its disciplines—to worship, to pray, to meditate, to study the Scriptures, to reflect on God's goodness and guidance, to repent. We cannot let war get inside us. There the peace that passes all understanding must reign.

After war begins, what form does faith take? The task of the Christian before, during, or after open militarism is no different than it was before the conflict: to reconcile people to God and with one another. This includes the enemy, those who promote militarism, and those who object to it. "Engaging in warfare strikes at the heart of discipleship and evangelism," writes John Drescher, in *Why I Am a Conscientious Objector.* "If I destroy a Christian, I kill the brother [or sister] for whom Scripture says I should lay down my life. If my enemy is a non-Christian, I destroy one for whom Christ died and take away any further opportunity to be a reconciler or to let him find salvation."

The gospel requires us to love our neighbors, not necessarily to like them. Killing is not loving. So grasp for opportunities for bringing together, even as others turn to hating, rejection, and division. Reconciliation is better than destruction. Because of the possibility of reconciliation we are not short-term kingdom workers. Reconciliation makes beginning over and over again possible.

Resist the temptation to cower in a corner like a hunted animal, nursing bitterness and hopelessness. Reach out creatively. A church with true spirituality is a creative church. A Christian with true spirituality is a creative person.

Committing Acts of Life

My daughter Christine, a parish nurse at St. Gertrude's Catholic Church in inner Chicago, expresses the thoughts of many when she writes, "It seems important to talk about how war information makes me feel—sad, angry, numb, lonely—so that the depression resulting from it does not become a downward spiral, but rather a time of reckoning from which I move on. It's like the whole country has been given a diagnosis of serious illness, someone told me, and we have the chance to figure out what is truly important. What do I value? What does this country value? What does God value? I don't have the complete answers, but it does seem important to me, in the face of acts of war, to commit acts of life."

Acts of war. Acts of life. Though we cannot control the first, we can determine the second. Our weapons are not smart bombs and Stealth fighters but the creative blend of life and love. To Christine, that means affirming the beauty of being alive, whether it is praying for peace in a church or at the federal building, calling a friend, singing a song, or being totally present to work.

It also means second-mile religion. Giving up at least one coat. Enlarging homes to accommodate the homeless and deprived. Grieving with families whose sons, daughters, husbands, and wives are overseas. To avoid involvement with life means being without moral and spiritual power. Acts of war must never overtake acts of life regardless how difficult the situation. Then Satan has completely defeated us.

In 1990, Nancy Cruzan's father petitioned the courts for the right to disconnect her life support systems because she had been comatose for several years. On Friday, December 21, 1990, he met briefly on the hospital steps in Mount Vernon, Missouri, with prolife protesters who were maintaining a round-the-clock vigil. He came to them to do more than talk. He brought the protesters a coffee pot, cups, and an extension cord. He knew what they needed on this shortest and perhaps coldest day of the year, writes Sharon Fish (*Christianity Today*, February 1991).

That coffee pot said more than had he argued with them. If conflict alienates us from those who differ from us, our pacifist stand is a tawdry ornament dangling from a worn string. This present conflict is our opportunity to escape the Vietnam era polarization.

Henri Nouwen tells a story how to know when the light of love has overcome the darkness of hatred. A rabbi asked his students, "How can we determine the hour of dawn, when the night ends and the day begins?"

One of his students suggested, "When from a distance you can distinguish between a dog and a sheep?" The rabbi answered, "No."

"Is it when one man can distinguish between a fig tree and grape vine?" asked a second student. The answer again was no.

"Please tell us the answer then," said the students.

"It is, then," said the wise teacher, "when you can look into the face of human beings and you have enough light [in you] to recognize them as your brothers and sisters. Up until then it is night and darkness is still with us." Only we, personally, know when our "peace position" draws us closer to others rather than creates chasms.

Trusting in God's Blessing

Conflict also compels us to think through our view of the nature of God. In this fast-forward age, many Christians believe in a prayer-answering God for objective reasons—to make life more comfortable. Prayer lists abound with requests for better health, more money to pay the bills, daily protection, well-behaved children, and occasionally a two-week summer trip. Some carry this "God-owes-this-to-me" attitude with them into their thinking about nonviolence. If they're fervent pacifists, surely God will respond by spreading lavish measures of peace and goodwill all around.

In Matthew 5 Jesus taught a mode of behavior but promised nothing in material returns or rewards, only greater spiritual strength and blessing. Commitment to nonviolence must be based on the conviction that the way of peace and love as Jesus taught it is right. It reflects God's holy nature. We hold to it not because we will benefit from it. One commentator of the 1960s peace movement, which evaporated when the results didn't pan out as hoped for, said, "One can't experiment with pacifism without being committed to it, because the ultimate commitment requires the giving of one's life."

God will ultimately honor faith in the sovereignty of God, but we don't know when. To interpret world events as if we fully understand them is to know something only God knows. Violence has embedded in it the seeds of its own destruction. Our task is to trust God because God is God and we are God's creation who owe our Creator our worship. It means trusting in the power of powerlessness even as others demand position, power, and authority. Some Jews rejected Christ because he did not come as a powerful earthly ruler. His reign did not promise to effect change quickly and effectively. History's moment of greatest weakness and greatest power was on the cross of Calvary.

Some writers solace us that a large enough number of pacifists in a country might affect government policy and their example might encourage similar nonconformity among individuals in the enemy nation. But we don't have the assurance that it will. The blacks who remained loyal and obedient to their masters during the Civil War were not necessarily rewarded with freedom. We hold to peace because we are co-workers in God's struggle with an evil and violent world. The outcome lies in the sovereignty of God, not in our presumptions.

For the clear vision of peace to shine in a dark world, it needs the polish provided by a humble spirit. In a crisis, people feel a tremendous need to do something open and tangible so that others can see their convictions. Some even pray their witness will have enough show-element to make the evening news. An Oprah Winfrey television show aired at the time of the outbreak of hostilities included guests with varying attitudes toward the Persian Gulf conflict. The show made the evening news, but only because it ended in a wild shouting match, voices getting louder and louder. It proved only the existence of much disagreement, much pain, and much blaming.

To successfully argue a theological position or to publicly protest yet remain humble is a difficult assignment, for one may become more concerned with having an impact on the public than with the meaning of the impact. And critics are quick to notice. Tom Shales, TV critic, writes that the new video version of John Lennon's repetitious protest song, "Give Peace a Chance," is produced by people who appear "to be thrilled with the wonder of their own virtue."

We can't make people think, believe, act the way we want them to. Thomas Merton writes, "If we love our own ideology and our own opinion instead of loving our brother [or sister], we will seek only to glorify our ideas and institutions and by that fact we will make community impossible" (*Faith and Violence*, University of Notre Dame, 1968). He suggests we ask the question: "Are you more concerned with your own 'good' conscience than with the good of the oppressed?" A humble person acknowledges different perspectives and is willing to study them. A humble person acknowledges his or her own lapses. A humble person courageously witnesses to Christ's love even if no television camera or bystanders are present. And when ridiculed, a humble person forgives and holds no grudges. On the cross, when the powers of evil seemed victorious, Jesus cried out, "Father, forgive them for they know not what they do." Peace-people have the courage to forgive.

Symbols of God's Love and Peace

What many people don't realize is that a great power, a great wealth of a nation, a people, the church, lies in its symbols. A symbol is often more powerful than the reality behind it. People rally behind symbols to bolster failing spirits. We need stronger and richer symbols to strengthen the image of the essence of nonviolent action "in the minds and memories of modern [humanity] not only as being conceivable and possible, but as a desirable alternative" to what people now consider the only realistic possibility, namely "political manipulation backed by force," states Merton. Over the years much preaching and teaching has become so analytical and propositional, even about peace, that our public witness lacks sufficient "soul-force" to capture the imagination of the people about the better way of love.

I cast about for suitable symbols. We can't compete with the flood of symbols of nationalistic and commercial efforts. Much of the confetti of bracelets, yellow ribbons, flags, banners, bumper stickers, buttons, T-shirts, and jewelry disappears once a war is over. The dove, long considered a peace symbol, has become a political symbol, so it has lost its power to speak in other arenas. An olive branch then? Or an oil lamp to symbolize the outpouring of God's Spirit and the need to let our lights shine? These and others have possibilities.

In organizing the civil rights peace marches, Martin Luther King, Jr., told the world that U.S. blacks had chosen another way, a better way. The strength of that symbol lay in the blacks' willingness to suffer imprisonment and physical violence. The symbol of Christ's love will only be as strong as our readiness to suffer for our convictions. Might this mean giving up our love affair with oil products? driving alone? lowering our passion for high levels of creature comforts and consumer products at the expense of justice in underdeveloped countries? rejecting our wholesale addiction to entertainment?

Is any symbol strong enough to carry the weight of Christ's love? Only one—the cross. The sacrifice on the cross is the sign of what God did with sin and evil and suffering. Sacrifice must become our symbol.

A powerful example of sacrificial love is Maximilian Kolbe, the prisoner in the Dachau concentration camp who willingly took the place of a man condemned to die. Among many cruel hardships, Kolbe once was beaten senseless, but even while sick, he accepted no privileges for himself. Whatever happened, he assured his fellow prisoners, love is stronger than hate. "Hatred is not creative." He knew he would not survive the camp, but he urged them to stay alive.

After his voluntary death, he became a powerful symbol in the struggle against evil. "The lunatic program of the Nazis was defeated by military might," wrote one observer, "but the deepest essence of the meaning of humanity was liberated neither by armies nor by politicians. The definitive answer was given by a Polish Franciscan, Father Maximilian Kolbe."

Yet something else is needed. No vision of love and peace grows bright until it has first been blurred by tears. Of sorrow. Of anger and frustration. Of repentance. So cry before God. Cry to God. Holler. Holler loudly. Tell God how you feel—lonely, angry, numb, sorrowing, disappointed in God's absence. The psalmist cried to God, "Why have you rejected us forever, O God?" He

---

Prayer for the Healing of the Nations

Lord, the nations of the earth lie sick and separated
from each other. Hear, O Lord, our prayers
for the healing of these lands and peoples we love.
Remove this illness so that, fully recovered
and restored to health, the nations of the earth
may live in colorful harmony and cooperation.

We trust fully in your divine power
to stir the latent healing powers on our planet,
and to remove all that causes dissension,
pain, war, and alienation.

Divine Healer and Lord of Wholeness,
together we place ourselves in your care.
Send your Holy Spirit to help us
create peace wherever people live,
and give a new face to this earth so dear to us.

Amen.

—*Christine Wiebe*

---

hurled angry invectives against the enemy and pled with God to
destroy those who sought his life. Yet even those harsh words
reveal faith in God because they are addressed to God.

In Psalm 137 the Jews asked the question, "How can we sing
the songs of the Lord in a foreign land?" That is also our question. Yet sing it we must. We sing the song of the Lord as a song of
defiance to show to whom we belong. "We aren't the property of
any passing 'powers-that-be,' " someone has said. We sing it to
sustain ourselves. We sing it to show our dissatisfaction with the
way things are. We sing to show that God is not through with the
human race yet.

We also sing the Lord's song as a gesture of hope for the
healing of the nations. Hope is waiting for God to act. Hope is
submitting to God to see what God will do through the conflict.

Hope leads out of lostness and loneliness, even like that of a child astray in the snow. Hope leads to praise of God. Selah.

Katie Funk Wiebe is professor emeritus at Tabor College, Hillsboro, Kansas, where she taught in the English department for twenty-three years. She is editor of Rejoice!, *an inter-Mennonite devotional publication, and also a free-lance writer, author of books and curriculum material.*

Questions for Discussion and Reflection

Chapter 1 What We Believe

1. Would you consider fleeing from one country to another rather than submit to joining the military?

2. Do you believe that participation in war is unacceptable for Mennonites? all Christians? all people, regardless of religion? Are there any "just" wars?

3. Is there any real difference between going to war or paying so that others may go to war?

4. What kinds of public acts of opposition to war are acceptable?

Chapter 2 Pacifism and Patriotism

1. Should the Christian pacifist "find ways to be a little patriotic" when a popular war is being fought?

2. How much loyalty should the Christian give the nation? At what point might the claims of the nation trespass upon the call and claims of God?

3. Longacre writes that feeding the hungry, laboring for justice, providing housing for the poor, and other acts of compassion serve the nation (and the world) as surely as the sacrifice others make of sending people off to war. Do you agree?

4. Is it appropriate to have flags and other patriotic symbols in the church building? If not, what symbols are appropriate?

Chapter 3   War's Impact on the Poor

1. How can nations share resources among all people in fair and equitable ways?

2. How do North American societies measure up against the biblical concept of shalom?

3. In what ways can the church listen to the message of the powerless and challenge society to solve domestic problems? What is the church's role in influencing the government to change policies in order to meet the needs of hurting people?

3. Brown writes that military spending takes money away from the poor, the homeless, the hungry. How much money does your community receive for the upkeep of military bases or from defense contracts? How could the same amount of money be spent to meet the basic needs of all citizens?

Chapter 4   Where Will War Lead Us?

1. Could civilization have developed without war? Could Adam and Eve have stayed in the Garden of Eden?

2. Have we improved in our ability to live in peace with our neighbors since the dawn of history?

3. Will we be able to adapt to the existence of weapons of mass destruction by controlling or eliminating their use?

Chapter 5   Living in the Global Community

1. Why does it seem to be so difficult for Jews, Christians, and Muslims to get along with each other? Can people of differing religions live together in peace?

2. How much priority should a developing country's human rights record be given when nations are deciding how to distribute food and medicine? economic aid? military assistance?

3. How ought Christians to respond when political leaders use religion to justify their actions?

4. What are some ways Christians can take the lead in increasing their understanding of other religions and cultures?

Chapter 6   Limited War in a Century of Total War

1. Look carefully at Juhnke's conditions for a total war. Did the conflict in the Persian Gulf fit these criteria?

2. How far should conscientious objectors go to avoid participating in acts that directly or indirectly aid a nation's war effort?

3. How do faithful Christians find their place in a society at war when the population is called upon to make few, if any, sacrifices for the war effort?

Chapter 7   The Economics of War

1. Harder says that North American countries were drawn into the Persian Gulf War primarily to protect access to cheap oil. Might we feel compelled to fight more natural resource wars in the future for much the same reason? What resources besides oil might our countries fight over?

2. Can a Christian work in a defense-related job and still be a pacifist?

3. What are some ways existing defense plants could be converted to peaceful uses?

4. What is the danger in a country being able to fight a short war (such as the war in the Persian Gulf) without causing major disruption to the nation's economy?

Chapter 8   Mass Media and War

1. How much freedom should journalists have in reporting from the front? Do you think people outside war zones generally see or hear the truth about the war?

2. What responsibility do reporters have to present dissenting points of view?

3. To whom do journalists owe their ultimate allegiance: the truth? the audience? their employers? their country?

4. Do you think the news media helped shape the way the people viewed the Persian Gulf War or did they simply report what was happening? Were the media biased for the war effort? against the war?

Chapter 9   War and the Elementary Classroom

1. How did your local school district react to the war in the Persian Gulf? Could you play a role in helping the schools be sensitive to all views about war?

2. What values are so universal that they can be taught in the public school classroom? Is peacemaking one of these values?

3. How would you respond to war-related school policies (such as wearing yellow or red, white, and blue ribbons; singing patriotic songs; writing letters to soldiers, etc.)?
   a. Do what is recommended.
   b. Silently do not comply.
   c. State your beliefs if asked.
   d. State you beliefs boldly at any time possible.

4. How can peacemakers avoid stereotyping and prejudice toward people who believe differently than they do?

Chapter 10   War, Peace, and the Workplace

1. Do people have to choose between personal convictions and relationships with co-workers? If yes, why? If no, why not?

2. What are some ways to deal with differences of opinion among co-workers?

3. What are some ways to keep from feeling overwhelmed by uncontrollable events in the world? What is the impact of these actions?

4. How do we deal with threatening situations? How do we deal with challenges? Can threats be turned into challenges?

Chapter 11   Peacemakers Confronted

1. Should dissent during wartime be considered treason? Is there ever a time when governments have the right to quiet their opposition?

2. How can Christian peacemakers communicate their convictions to a population that isn't interested in hearing anything negative about the war effort?

3. How can Christian pacifists confront the intimidation to silence without contributing to provocation?

Chapter 12   Becoming Friends with the Enemy

1. How can we develop critical thinking so we will not be swept along by government pronouncements or by public opinion?

2. How can people of peace promote a wider appreciation of the sacredness of all humanity, regardless of racial or ethnic background?

3. Do Christians have enemies? How can Christians reach out to people whom the government considers to be the enemy?

4. What are some ways people of peace can work at undoing racist attitudes within themselves? within the home? within the church? within the community?

Chapter 13   Crisis Care for Young Children

1. What are some ways adults can help young children understand the reality of war without causing undue fear or anger?

2. What are some ways to involve children in active peacemaking?

3. Adults cannot shield children from all the violence and conflict in the world. How can children be helped to cope with their fear and concern for safety?

Chapter 14   Empowering Teenagers for Peacemaking

1. How can your church encourage youth to become interested in peacemaking when there are seemingly no urgent reasons to discuss peace issues?

2. Youth are aware of violence and conflict in the world around them. How can they be helped to cope with their fear and concerns?

3. In what ways can youth be sensitized to injustice in their communities and in the world?

4. Who are role models for youth searching for ways to work for peace and justice?

5. Bergen concludes that the war in the Persian Gulf could not have happened if youth and adults in North American churches had been committed to peace and had voiced their concerns in the months leading up to the war. Do you agree or disagree? Why?

Chapter 15   Young Adults and War: The Burdening of a Generation

1. Are Jesus' teachings too idealistic and archaic for the real world?

2. How can young adults be challenged to respond to issues of peace and justice?

3. Keeler writes that just as the Christian faith is always one generation away from extinction, even more so is the peace doctrine of the church. Do you agree or disagree? Why?

4. For some young adults, military service seems to be the best choice for job training or to earn money for college. How ought Christian pacifists to respond to young adults who choose this option?

Chapter 16   Five Congregations Respond to Conflict

1. Several pastors wrote that prayer is the most important work that God's people can do for peace. Do you agree or disagree?

2. What are some ways your congregation has responded to conflict within the fellowship? in the community? in the world?

3. How does your congregation teach peace and peacemaking to the children of the church?

4. How might a pacifist church minister to a son or daughter of the congregation who is a member of the armed forces? What response might the congregation have for the family of the soldier?

Chapter 17   When Faith Comes Under Fire

1. How can Christian pacifists answer those who believe that refraining from violence allows evil to go unchecked?

2. Is it possible to love one's enemies and still be at war with them?

3. How can the church become the reconciling community of God?

4. Wiebe writes that we cannot always control acts of war, but that we can determine acts of life. What acts of life can people of faith commit in the face of conflict?

5. What are some ways people of faith can practice sacrificial love?

Selected Bibliography

Chapter 6: Limited War in a Century of Total War

Dyer, Gwynn. *War.* Chicago: Dorsey Press, 1985.

Kennan, George. *American Diplomacy.* New York: New American Library, 1951.

Weigley, Russell. *The American Way of War.* New York: Macmillan, 1973.

Chapter 7: The Economics of War

DuBoff, Richard B. "What Military Spending Really Costs." *Challenge,* September/October 1989.

Melman, Seymour. *The Permanent War Economy.* New York: Simon and Schuster, 1974, revised edition 1985.

Mennonite Central Committee, U.S. Peace Section. *Washington Memo* (bimonthly publication).

Renner, Michael. "Swords into Plowshares: Converting to a Peace Economy." Worldwatch Institute, Paper 96, June 1990.

Chapter 11: Peacemakers Confronted

Arnett, Ronald C. *Dwell in Peace: Applying Nonviolence to Everyday Relationships.* Elgin, Illinois: Brethren Press, 1980.

Bondurant, Joan V. *Conquest of Violence: The Gandhian Philosophy of Conflict.* Berkeley, California: University of California Press, 1971.

Kreider, Robert S. and Rachel Waltner Goossen. *When Good People Quarrel: Studies of Conflict Resolution.* Scottdale: Herald Press, 1989.

Ruth-Heffelbower, Duane. *The Anabaptists Are Back: Making Peace in a Dangerous World.* Scottdale: Herald Press, 1991.

Sider, Ronald J. *Nonviolence: The Invincible Weapon?* Dallas: Word Publishing, 1989.

Chapter 13: Crisis Care for Young Children

Rogers, Fred and Hedda Bluestone Sharapan. "Helping Parents, Teachers, and Care Givers Deal with Children's Concerns About War." Pittsburgh, Pennsylvania: Family Communications, Inc., 1991. "When Children Ask About War." New Windsor, Maryland: The Cooperative Disaster Child Care Program, 1991.

Chapter 14: Empowering Teenagers for Peacemaking

Brueggemann, Walter. *The Bible Makes Sense.* Winona, Minnesota: St. Mary's College Press, 1977.

Strommen, Merton P. *Five Cries of Youth.* San Francisco: Harper & Row, revised 1988.

Yoder, Perry B. *Shalom: The Bible's Word for Salvation, Justice, and Peace.* Newton: Faith and Life Press, 1987.

Zimmerman, Jon. "A New Reason to Serve." *With,* March 1991.

Mennonites—
Who Are They?

All the authors in this book are members of churches or related to institutions connected with the Christian community of believers known as Mennonites. With roots in the Reformation and Anabaptist movements of the sixteenth century, Mennonites seek to live in ways that are consistent with, and based on, the teachings of Jesus Christ.

Characteristics of this faith include commitment to believer's baptism, Christian discipleship, service to the world, active peacemaking, and a Scripture-based faith. Passages in the New Testament such as the Sermon on the Mount (Matthew 4-6) and the Great Commission (Matthew 28:19, 20) have taken on special importance for Mennonites as they seek to incorporate aspects of faith as modeled by Christ into their everyday lives.

The Mennonite commitment to peacemaking, social justice, and service in our world is evidenced by the group's identification as a historic peace church. Denominational relief, mission, and service agencies join the internationally recognized Mennonite Central Committee in actively ministering to a hurting and needy world. It is the goal of Mennonites to serve and love others as Christ has loved us.

For no one can lay any foundation other than the one that has been laid; that foundation is Jesus Christ. (1 Corinthians 3:11 NRSV)

Susan E. Janzen, Editor
April, 1991